# The ROAD

*Releasing the Power of*

# MOST

*Contentment in Your Life*

# TRAVELED

# Robert Jeffress

BROADMAN
& HOLMAN
PUBLISHERS

D0249613

Printed in the United States of America

4262-66
0-8054-6266-X

Published by
Broadman & Holman Publishers
Nashville, Tennessee

Dewey Decimal Classification: 248.842
Subject Heading: Christian Life/Men—Religious Life
Library of Congress Card Catalog Number: 95-46535

Unless otherwise noted, Scripture quotations are from NASB, New American Standard Bible, © the Lockman Foundation, 1960, 1962, 1963, 1968, 1971, 1972, 1973, 1975, 1977; used by permission. Others passages are from NIV, the Holy Bible, New International Version, copyright © 1973, 1978, 1984 by International Bible Society; TLB, The Living Bible, copyright © Tyndale House Publishers, Wheaton, Ill., 1971, used by permission; and RSV, Revised Standard Version of the Bible, copyrighted 1946, 1952, © 1971, 1973.

Library of Congress Cataloging-in-Publication Data

Jeffress, Robert, 1955–
    The road most traveled : releasing the extraordinary power of
    contentment in your life / Robert Jeffress.
        p.   cm.
    ISBN 0-8054-6266-X
    1. Contentment—Religious aspects—Christianity.   2. Men—
Religious life.   I. Title.
BV4647.C7J44     1996
248.8'42—dc20                                                95-46535
                                                               CIP

00  99  98  97  96  5  4  3  2  1

To Bobby Albert, Jerry Broadway, Ed Callender, Clay Clark, Leroy Daniel, Bob Foley, Al Flack, Jim Ginnings, Eddie Huffman, E. V. Johnson, Mark Lovvorn, Leon Mallonee, Jerry Mathis, C. D. Rogers, Ben Shelton, Ray Smith, Bill Spears, Jack Wallace, Harold Warren, Lane West, Stan West, and Stanley Williamson, whose generous gift and encouragement made my journey down *The Road Most Traveled* much easier.

# CONTENTS

# CHAPTER ONE

## The Road Most Traveled

Steve could not understand how he had gotten where he was. The product of a strong Christian home, Steve had dedicated his life to Christ at an early age. He had a deep interest in spiritual things and even occasionally wondered if he should become a pastor. But he never felt "the call." That was all right. There wasn't that much money in the ministry, anyway. And Steve's goal had always been to make a *lot* of money. As a teenager, he had developed a taste for the "finer" things in life: designer clothes, luxury automobiles, exotic trips, gorgeous girlfriends. He knew that his ticket to acquiring those things would be a business degree in college and a career in finance.

After obtaining his undergraduate degree from a respected university, Steve stayed an extra two years to earn his master's degree. He then found both a job in an investment firm and a beautiful wife—all in the same year. He was on his way.

Steve's first crisis occurred two years into his marriage. The firm where he worked became the victim of a takeover. In the downsizing of the organization, Steve lost his job. Fortunately, he was able to find work with a local real estate broker. In addition to a bigger salary, Steve was provided with a luxury automobile. As he drove around on the weekends in his shiny red Lincoln with his beautiful wife sitting by his side, he thought, *Life doesn't get much better than this.*

Then one morning, out of nowhere, his wife announced she was leaving him. Steve was devastated. He tried to reason with her, but she was not interested. Later he discovered that she had been having numerous affairs behind his back. Although that revelation answered several questions, it only deepened the hurt. Steve's strong religious beliefs against divorce had caused him to think he was immune from that possibility. Steve became an unwilling party to what he had so often condemned.

For the next year Steve tried to work himself out of his depression over his failed marriage. During that time he met a wonderfully committed Christian girl named Kathy. They fell in love and married. However, shortly after they married a downturn in oil prices in Texas hammered the real estate market. Once again, Steve lost his job. After months of searching, Steve finally found employment as a teacher, earning about one-half his previous salary. His low salary necessitated his wife's working nights at a video store. She worked all night, he worked all day—not exactly the formula for a happy marriage.

Although finances were tight, Steve and Kathy desperately wanted a child. Using some money he had stashed away during better days, Steve figured out a way that he and Kathy could reduce their monthly expenses, and she could stay home to be a full-time homemaker. All they needed was a baby.

But that, too, became a problem. Medical difficulties made it impossible for Kathy to conceive a child naturally. After praying about the situation, Steve and Kathy borrowed $14,000 for an in vitro fertilization procedure. It failed. Then they borrowed another $12,000 to adopt a baby boy. For a time, the new addition to the family provided a much-needed diversion for Steve's life. But now the newness has worn off, and Steve is back to living an ordinary life.

Steve is not the typical male in a mid-life crisis. He is not thinking about leaving his family, having an affair, or even buying a red convertible—not yet, anyway. But as Steve honestly evaluates his life, he realizes he is in a far different place than where he thought he would be.

- He is stuck in a job in which he has no chance for a significant promotion.
- He is earning considerably less than he had a decade earlier.
- He is deeply in debt.
- He is the victim of one failed marriage.
- He will never be able to have a child of his own.

## THE STIRRINGS OF DISCONTENT

Steve is the victim of some extraordinary circumstances that have resulted in—not a terrible life—but an *ordinary* life. Gone are the dreams of a fast-track career, a large income, and a model family.

Is his present situation the result of wrong decisions, God's judgment, or just plain bad luck? Is there anything he could do to change his circumstances, or is he the victim of a supernatural plan for a mediocre life? Steve thinks about these questions often.

A time comes in every man 's life when he wakes up and realizes that he is not married to Cindy Crawford, he will never make the Fortune 400 list, and he probably won't be interviewed on "Focus on the Family" as a model father. Is a man's lack of achievement in life the result of disobedience, slothfulness, or misfortune? Or, are his circumstances a part of God's sovereign plan for his life?

Every Wednesday morning I teach a group of several hundred men on issues that relate to the male gender: how to be a loving husband, how to be a spiritual leader in the home, how to preserve your family against a pagan culture, and a variety of other topics.

My teaching mirrors what you find in most Christian men's books: the duties of a Christian man.

But as I talk with many of these men individually, I have discovered that they are wrestling with more basic issues. They know they should love their wives, but many wonder if they even have the right wife. They understand they should be better fathers, but they are afraid they have already made so many mistakes that they are doomed to failure. They believe they should have a closer relationship with God, but in their hearts they resent God for the hand He has dealt them in life.

*The Road Most Traveled* deals with the most basic issue in a man's life: contentment. Until a man can make peace with the unchangeable circumstances, choices, and even mistakes of his life, he will never be emotionally or spiritually free to perform the duties outlined by so many books. *The Road Most Traveled* is for anyone who is beginning to feel the stirrings of discontent about his life situation. You may be

- a manager who feels stuck in your job. Your chances for a promotion are slim, and you feel you are too old to switch professions. Should you have pursued a different career?

- a husband who married your high school sweetheart and now fear you may have made a mistake. Should you have held out for someone else?

- the pastor of a church in a deteriorating town of three thousand who is discouraged over not filling your sanctuary each week. Is this really God's will for your life?

Whatever your particular situation is, you realize you are not where you thought you would be by now. Unfulfilled dreams are becoming more of a reality with each passing year.

## "IF I HAD MY LIFE TO LIVE OVER . . ."

Take a moment to complete the following survey. How would you rate your satisfaction level with each of these life areas?

(1 is the lowest; 10 is the highest)

| | | | | | | | | | | |
|---|---|---|---|---|---|---|---|---|---|---|
| Marriage | 1 | 2 | 3 | 4 | 5 | 6 | 7 | 8 | 9 | 10 |
| Children | 1 | 2 | 3 | 4 | 5 | 6 | 7 | 8 | 9 | 10 |
| Job | 1 | 2 | 3 | 4 | 5 | 6 | 7 | 8 | 9 | 10 |
| Finances | 1 | 2 | 3 | 4 | 5 | 6 | 7 | 8 | 9 | 10 |
| Spiritual life | 1 | 2 | 3 | 4 | 5 | 6 | 7 | 8 | 9 | 10 |
| Physical Appearance | 1 | 2 | 3 | 4 | 5 | 6 | 7 | 8 | 9 | 10 |

Now grade yourself. (If your score is: 0–25, you're closer to a red convertible than you think; 26–47, there are definitely some unresolved issues in your life; 48–60, congratulations! You can now close the book and give it to a depressed friend.)

Take time to think about the following statements. Although your answers cannot be scored, they will help to surface some issues in your life that we will deal with in this book.

- I would be much happier if I had more _____
  _____
  _____.

- My life would be much more pleasurable if I had less ____
  _____
  _____.

- As a child/teenager, my biggest dream was to _____
  _____
  _____.

- The biggest mistake I ever made in life was _____
  _____
  _____.

- If money were no object, I would _____
  _____
  _____.

- My ideal career would be _____
  _____
  _____.

- If I could select one person in my circle of friends or acquaintances with whom I could switch places, it would be

    _____

    _____ .

## IS "MORE" OR "DIFFERENT" WRONG?

I remember hearing a seminar speaker ask the question, "If you could change one thing about your physical appearance, what would it be?" It was a trick question. The leader went on to say that if you were able to answer that question, it meant you had a poor self-image and did not accept yourself as God made you. Shame on you.

I am not suggesting that if you filled in the blanks to the above statements, you do not accept God's plan for your life. But I do believe we make a fundamental mistake when we assume that satisfaction in life is just beyond where we are.

A rabbi once approached a member of his congregation and said, "Whenever I see you, you're always in a hurry. Tell me, where are you running all the time?" The man answered, "I'm running after success, I'm running after fulfillment, I'm running after the reward for all my hard work." The rabbi responded, "That's a good answer if you assume that all those blessings are somewhere ahead of you, trying to elude you, and if you run fast enough, you may catch up with them. But isn't it possible that those blessings are behind you, that they are looking for you, and the more you run, the harder you make it for them to find you?"[1]

Most men I know are running after something. Some are running harder than others, but most of us believe that true satisfaction in life is just beyond our grasp. If we run hard enough we might just be able to seize it. Robert Hastings imaginatively expresses the error of such thinking in his work "The Station":

> Tucked away in our subconscious is an idyllic vision. We
> see ourselves on a long trip that spans the continent. We
> are traveling by train. Out the windows we drink in

the passing scene of cars on nearby highways, of children waving at a crossing, of cattle grazing on a distant hillside, of smoke pouring from a power plant, of row upon row of corn and wheat, of flatlands and valleys, of mountains and rolling hillsides, of city skylines and village halls.

But uppermost in our minds is the final destination. On a certain day at a certain hour we will pull into the station. Bands will be playing and flags waving. Once we get there so many wonderful dreams will come true and the pieces of our lives will fit together like a completed jigsaw puzzle. How restlessly we pace the aisles, damning the minutes for loitering—waiting, waiting, waiting for the station.

"When we reach the station, that will be it!" we cry. "When I'm 18." "When I buy a new 450 SL Mercedes Benz!" "When I put the last kid through college." "When I have paid off the mortgage!" "When I get a promotion." "When I reach the age of retirement, I shall live happily after that!"

Sooner or later we must realize there is no station, no place to arrive at once and for all. The true joy of life is the trip. The station is only a dream. It constantly outdistances us. . . .

So, stop pacing the aisles and counting the miles. Instead, climb more mountains, eat more ice cream, go barefoot more often, swim more rivers, watch more sunsets, laugh more, cry less. Life must be lived as we go along. The station will come soon enough.[2]

Maybe you are one of those people who have built your happiness in life upon some future, extraordinary event. "When _____ happens, I will finally be happy." However, the truth is that momentous events in life are few and far between. Only a handful of us will ever ascend to the presidency of a major corporation, earn six-figure incomes, become famous for some outstanding achievement, escape some problem with our children, or enjoy a perfect marriage. Most of us are destined to live ordinary lives. One writer has described the ordinary life for a man this way:

> The straight life for a working man is . . . pulling your tired frame out of bed, five days a week, fifty weeks out of the year. It is earning a two-week vacation in August, and choosing a trip that will please the kids. The straight life is spending your money wisely when you'd rather indulge in a new whatever; it is taking your son bike riding on Saturday when you want so badly to watch the baseball game; it is cleaning out the garage on your day off after working sixty hours the prior week. The straight life is coping with head colds and engine tune-ups and crab grass and income-tax forms.[3]

That is the life most of us live. And that's all right. The premise of this book is that lasting satisfaction in life does not come from extraordinary events, but by learning to appreciate the unchangeable circumstances, choices, and even mistakes that shape our destiny.

*The Road Most Traveled* will show you how to find contentment in your present life situation, rather than in some mythical and distant "station." Specifically, this book will help you

- learn to trust in God's unique plan for your life.
- distinguish between the changeable and unchangeable aspects of your life.
- see how God can use your mistakes to bring about His will.
- appreciate the family God has given you.
- forgive people who have hurt you.
- prepare for your inevitable death.

Let me add one other benefit of this book. Learning to make peace with your present life situation will also help you avoid making mistakes in life—mistakes like those of the man you are about to meet.

## FOR FURTHER REFLECTION

1. What aspects of Steve's situation are you able to identify with?


2. What did the survey on page 5 reveal to you about your level of contentment? Which life area are you least satisfied with? Why?


3. Did you find it easy or difficult to answer the questions on page 5? How much difference is there between where you are and where you would like to be in life?


4. Describe your ideal vision of "the station" for your life. Have you ever experienced a disappointment that suggested no such "station" exists? Explain.


5. Complete the following sentence: I hope this book will help me to _____

_____.

# CHAPTER TWO

## Mid-Life Mess-Up

In her landmark book on the subject of mid-life transitions, Nancy Mayer relates an interview with a forty-three-year-old man named Harry:

> The way I feel right now, I guess, is trapped. By all the pressures and responsibilities. By my job and the office and Sue and the kids and my father. . . . But what can I do? I can't just quit my job or break up my marriage or go running off to some South Seas island. That's ridiculous.
>
> Sometimes I think about buying a farm, living out in the country where it's peaceful. I did that one summer when I was a kid, worked on a farm. Had a ball, too. But that's just a pipe dream now. I'll never really do it.

So I just keep on doing the same . . . things every day. I run to the office, then I run to the hospital [to check on my father] . . . and then I run back to the house. . . . I feel like I'm always running, but I don't even know what I'm chasing after anymore. It's like being on a . . . treadmill. You just feel trapped, you know?[1]

Has your life turned into a treadmill with no possible way off getting off? Do you ever dream of running away from all of your present responsibilities and starting over? What is about the mid-life years that make a man especially susceptible to discontent? As we begin our journey down "the road most traveled," we are going to look at one of the most celebrated figures of the Old Testament—one who allowed discontent to almost destroy his life.

Whenever we think of Moses, we picture the mighty leader of Israel who stood before Pharaoh, pronouncing ten plagues upon Egypt. Images of the exodus, the parting of the Red Sea, and Charlton Heston come to mind. That's Moses. A man who bounced from one success to another. Right? Wrong! A closer examination reveals that Moses started out well and he ended fairly well. But the middle years of his of life were marked by tremendous failure and severe questions about God. Moses messed up in mid-life.

Men today confront many of the same pressures during the mid-life years (usually between thirty-eight and fifty) that caused Moses to make a wrong choice that forever marked his life. Moses' experience helps us identify—and hopefully avoid—the traps in mid-life that can rob us of contentment.

## FROM THE PALACE TO THE PRAIRIE

The first forty years of Moses' life are compressed into ten short verses in Exodus. In order to escape Pharaoh's persecution against all of the newborn males of Israel, Moses' mother placed him in a wicker basket and floated it down the Nile. Notice the overriding providence of God in Moses' early life:

Then the daughter of Pharaoh came down to bathe at the Nile, with her maidens walking alongside the Nile; and she saw the basket among the reeds and sent her maid, and she brought it to her. When she opened it, she saw the child, and behold, the boy was crying. And she had pity on him and said, "This is one of the Hebrews' children." Then his sister said to Pharaoh's daughter, "Shall I go and call a nurse for you from the Hebrew women, that she may nurse the child for you?" And Pharaoh's daughter said to her, "Go ahead." So the girl went and called the child's mother. . . . And the child grew, and she brought him to Pharaoh's daughter, and he became her son. And she named him Moses, and said, "Because I drew him out of the water" (Ex. 2:5–10).

The only other word the Bible gives us about Moses' first forty years of life comes from Acts 7:21–22: "After he had been exposed, Pharaoh's daughter took him away, and nurtured him as her own son. And Moses was educated in all the learning of the Egyptians, and he was a man of power in words and deeds." Moses was definitely a "comer." He was on the way to the top; that is, until he made one wrong decision that cost him everything.

Now it came about in those days, when Moses had grown up, that he went out to his brethren and looked on their hard labors; and he saw an Egyptian beating a Hebrew, one of his brethren. So he looked this way and that, and when he saw there was no one around, he struck down the Egyptian and hid him in the sand. And he went out the next day, and behold, two Hebrews were fighting with each other; and he said to the offender, "Why are you striking your companion?" But he said, "Who made you a prince or a judge over us? Are you intending to kill me, as you killed the Egyptian?" Then Moses was afraid, and said, "Surely the matter has become known." When Pharaoh heard of this matter, he tried to kill Moses. But Moses fled from the presence of Pharaoh and settled in the land of Midian; and he sat down by a well (Ex. 2:11–15).

In an instant, Moses had allowed his temper to get the best of him and he lost everything. His status changed overnight from "future ruler" to "fugitive." What did Moses think about as he stopped to get his breath by that well in the desert region of Midian? I'm sure that the heat and the discomfort of the desert made him long for the comforts of Pharaoh's palace. But I imagine that in the quietness of the desert he was forced to come to grips with reality. He had no one to blame for his condition but himself. His life had unraveled like a cheap sweater because of a mistake *he* had made.

When did Moses make this choice that destroyed his life? We find the answer in Acts 7: "But when he was approaching *the age of forty* [emphasis mine], it entered his mind to visit his brethren, the sons of Israel. And when he saw one of them being treated unjustly, he defended him and took vengeance for the oppressed by striking down the Egyptian. And he supposed that his brethren understood that God was granting them deliverance through him; but they did not understand" (vv. 23–25).

It was at the age of forty, that Moses became dissatisfied with his life's situation. And you can understand why. After all, God had promised Moses that He would deliver Israel from their Egyptian bondage. But nothing was happening. Forty years had passed and Moses felt trapped in his situation. So Moses decided he needed to help God fulfill His promise (*always* a bad decision—just ask Abraham).

Maybe you can think of men you know in the mid-life years who allowed a wrong choice to destroy their lives:

- A man who invests his life savings in a "guaranteed" deal, only to lose everything he has.
- A husband who forfeits his wife and children for a woman half his age.
- A successful manager who gives up a well-paying job for no other reason than he is not "fulfilled" any longer.

At the bottom of each of these wrong choices is the very real feeling of discontent—dissatisfaction with our economic status, or our family, or our work. Notice when that dissatisfaction is most likely to come—in the mid-life years.

## MIDDLE-AGE CRAZIES

When I was pastoring in a smaller community, I remember that whenever a man would get a new hairstyle, or trade in his pickup for a sports car, or trade in his wife for a girlfriend, people would roll their eyes and say, "He's got a case of the middle-age crazies." There comes a time in every man's life when he is prone to reevaluate his life and make radical choices. We commonly refer to that period of time as a mid-life crisis.

Some have referred to the mid-life crisis as "male menopause"—though there is no evidence to suggest that men experience the same kind of hormonal irregularities as women do. Some believe that the whole idea of a mid-life crisis is the result of the overactive imagination of a group of psychologists (probably male) invented to sell books, promote costly therapy, or provide intellectual alibis for a man's misbehavior.

Part of the skepticism about a definable mid-life transition period is due to the absence of universal physical or psychological markers that signal the beginning and end of such a transition period. If, at age forty, every man suddenly lost all of his hair, we could say, "Poor George has begun his mid-life transition." Likewise, if on his fiftieth birthday every man automatically purchased a diamond necklace for his wife to demonstrate his renewed devotion, we could say, "Thank goodness, Bert has now completed his mid-life transition."

Though such definitive external signs do not exist, the mid-life transition is a very real phenomenon. Dr. Daniel Levinson and a team of researchers from Yale University did a study on mid-life crisis involving a number of men between the ages of thirty-five and forty-five. These are the general conclusions reached in their study:

- All men go through a mid-life crisis in one form or another. Most men experience it at forty; others in their thirties; and still others in their fifties.

- For some men, the mid-life transition goes smoothly; others experience tremendous upheavals in their lives. This transition period is marked by doubts about work, family, and goals. Although this period of doubt is disturbing, it is a necessary part of normal personality development.

- Not only is the mid-life transition predictable, but it is *desirable*. This period in a man's life allows for growth and changes that were never before possible. It is possible for a man to successfully navigate through this period of life and experience even greater fulfillment in his work, family, and other relationships.

- No matter when this mid-life crisis occurs and what the result is, it is a turning point in every man's life that will tremendously impact his future.[2]

## WHY WE DO THE THINGS WE DO

What is it about these mid-life years that cause a man to reevaluate every part of his life? Let's look at five factors that contribute to the mid-life reevaluation (a term I prefer to "crisis").

### Physiological Changes

Nancy Mayer may be a woman, but she is certainly aware of the physical symptoms that befall a man in mid-life:

This is the time of life, for example, when a man begins to worry about his body. Suddenly he suffers from prostate troubles and pulled muscles. Suddenly he needs glasses or root canal work. His cholesterol count goes up, his energy level down. His body is less reliable on the tennis court, less resilient under stress. He can no longer work such long hours or travel at his usual hectic pace.

He finds it maddening, this loss of control. He feels that his body has betrayed him.

High blood pressure develops and so do ulcers. Psychosomatic illnesses erupt: A man is suddenly beset by chronic fatigue, acute indigestion, mysterious backaches, painful joints, and migraine headaches. He complains a lot or even becomes hypochondriac, convinced that every cold is the forerunner of pneumonia, every pain the sign of cancer, and every rapid heartbeat the precursor of a coronary.

Often he panics over his sexual performance and suffers from bouts of impotence. He may become lethargic about sex and cut down his activity. Or do just the opposite, pursuing new sexual conquests with a vengeance. He jokes about sex compulsively, develops a sudden interest in X-rated films, or brags outrageously about his exploits.

To confirm his sexual appeal he may try to regain a youthful image by changing his appearance. He grows a beard or mustache, gets his hair styled or dyed. He buys a toupee, undergoes a hair transplant, or gets rid of his wrinkles and jowls by plastic surgery. He may also change his style of dress.[3]

Dr. Levinson, in his book *The Seasons of a Man's Life,* notes that although a man's physical capabilities do not decline dramatically during this period, the changes are enough to significantly alarm him: "Although he is not literally close to death or undergoing severe bodily decline, he typically experiences these changes as a fundamental threat. It is as though he were on the threshold of senility and even death."[4]

## Increased Responsibilities

A man entering the mid-life years finds himself with increasing responsibilities in every area of life.

*Increased Work.* The man who spends his late twenties and thirties planting the seeds of success in his career many times finds those seeds beginning to bear fruit as he enters mid-life: the lawyer reaches partnership status, the manager finally becomes a junior executive, the writer signs a contract for his first novel, the pastor is called to his first multi-staff church. These are the opportunities the man has been waiting for, and he feels he cannot squander them.

*Adolescent Children.* At a time when a man is facing increasing responsibilities in his work, he is also responsible to help navigate his children through the storms of adolescence. The son or daughter whose most difficult choice was who to invite to spend the night next Friday now faces choices about premarital sex, drugs, college, and a career.

*Aging Parents.* As a man's children are coming into adolescence and adulthood, his parents are becoming more like children. Increasing senility, physical incapacitation, or even the death of one parent cause a man to have to devote more and more time to the care of those who once cared for him. He is, in effect, the father to two generations.

*Community Responsibilities.* A man in mid-life is also expected to give something back to the organizations that have served him through the years. As older men increasingly move off the scene and into retirement, younger men are called upon to use their "free time" to serve as deacons or elders in their church, coaches of their children's teams, members of the school board, or leaders in civic organizations.

And so the man who reaches the mid-life years finds himself bombarded with increasing responsibilities in every life area. There is no end to the demands of work, family, and social responsibilities. No wonder that so many men fantasize about running off to a South Seas island.

### Realities of Work

The other day an associate of mine in his early forties commented, "I was talking with my wife last night and said, 'Honey, do you realize that we are making as much money now as we will probably ever make.' It was kind of depressing." My first reaction was to say, "Oh, no, that's not true. This is America. You are supposed to move higher and higher up the ladder of success until you reach the top of your profession. You have an entire life ahead of you in which to achieve."

Yet the truth was he probably had reached the top of his profession. He was a minister in a church larger than about 98 percent of the rest of the churches in America. Sure, there are a handful of churches larger, but there is no guarantee *he* would be called to one of them. In fact, every year that passed lessened the chance that he would move "upward."

That's the reality most men in mid-life face. One reason this period is so traumatic is that it represents the time of judgment on our entire career. In his twenties and thirties a man can rationalize his lack of success by telling himself that he "still has time." He can comfort himself by knowing that his peers are advancing no more quickly than he is. He can imagine that he is sowing seeds that will produce success in the years ahead.

But when a man reaches forty, it is a different story. If he has not "made it" by this point, he probably never will. Studies show that few men ever move up the organizational ladder past forty. Thus, the man in mid-life must face the fact that his dreams of achievement were just that—dreams. No wonder this period of time is called a "crisis."

## Futility of Success

Someone has said that there are only two tragedies in life: the first is not getting what you want; the second is getting it. Many times the man in mid-life *does* achieve the things he has been striving for during the last decade of his life—the house, the two cars, the management position, the large investment portfolio— only to discover that there is a greater void in his life.

I love goals. I have a folder that contains my written goals for the last fifteen years. I remember sitting down in the lobby of Houston Hobby airport ten years ago and writing specific goals for every area of my life: my family, my writing career, my net worth, the size of church I wanted to pastor, and on down the line. Recently I pulled out that sheet of paper and realized that I have exceeded those goals—some of them by a long shot. But am I more content than I was ten years ago? Hardly. In fact, realizing that I had met all of my goals only motivated me to write down ten more goals for the next five years of my life. Success is like saltwater—it only increases our thirst for more. Hugh Prather's words come to mind:

> The number of things just outside the perimeter of my financial reach remains constant no matter how much my financial condition improves. With each increase in my income a new perimeter forms and I experience the same relative sense of lack. I believe that I know the specific amount needed that would allow me to have or do these few things I can't quite afford, and if my income would increase by that much I would then be happy. Yet when the increase comes, I find that I am still discontent because from my new financial position I can now see a whole new set of things I don't have. The problem will be solved when I accept that happiness is a present attitude, not a future condition.[5]

Prather's words about financial success can be applied to accomplishments in every life area. The wisest man who ever lived had it right when he wrote, "And all that my eyes desired I did not refuse them. I did not withhold my heart from any pleasure, for my heart was pleased because of all my labor and this was my reward for all my labor. Thus I considered all my activities which my hands had done and the labor which I had exerted, and behold all was vanity and striving after wind and there was no profit under the sun" (Eccl. 2:10–11).

### Inevitability of Death

All of these pressures that cause a middle-aged man to reevaluate his life are secondary to the core issue: his approaching death.

The man in mid-life realizes that he has less time in front of him than behind him. And his remaining time is slipping away quickly.

Recently I saw an ad for a new device called The Timisis Lifetime Display. It is a digital clock that does more than tell time. By entering your current age and gender, you can see how much time you have left to live—second by second. Listen to what the ad promises: "Timisis, your personal LifeClock enables you to see time as a gift and motivates you to live your life to the fullest. An average lifetime lasts 678,900 hours or 2.4 billion seconds. . . .The Timisis Lifetime Display shows you the most profound number you will ever see . . . your lifetime. Enjoy Timisis. After all, it's the Time of Your Life."[6]

If you are not inclined to spend $99.95 for this gadget, you can measure your remaining time on earth by listening to one forty-seven year-old male talking to his son: "Every single day is important, whereas before it wasn't. I told my son . . . life is like a clock. We're born at six o'clock in the morning, and at six o'clock in the evening we die. So I've had breakfast, I've had lunch, and I'm at about two-fifteen on the clock of life. I've got one great big dinner left to order. That's it! When it becomes six o' clock I lower my head with the sun and I'm gone."[7]

When I came across the above quote, I could not keep it to myself. So I called my best friend (also in his early forties). We both noted how our wives do not share this same preoccupation with the inevitability of death. Our wives tend to view their lives in terms of major events: marriage, the birth of our children, their beginning school, and so on. But for us, the mid-life years represent a radical transformation in how we view time. We no longer calculate time in terms of the years since we were born; now our focus is on the years we have left.

I do not believe my friend and I are unique. The deafening sound of the ticking clock is *the* major catalyst for many men to reexamine every aspect of their lives:

- Do I want to spend the rest of my life with my wife?
- Why are my children not any more responsive to me than they are?

- Am I laboring in the career I want for the rest of my working years?
- Do I *really* believe the moral and spiritual truths I have espoused most of my life?
- Is there another location in the country where I would rather live?
- Why haven't I achieved as much as some of my peers?

The mid-life transition is a pause—a necessary pause—in a man's life to ask some of these basic questions. However, a man does not have to completely shipwreck his life during this mid-life reevaluation. It is possible to come through this period of life stronger than when we entered it—as long as we learn the "secret" we will examine in the next chapter.

## FOR FURTHER REFLECTION

1. In a sentence, summarize the cause of Moses' frustration that led him to make such a poor choice.

2. Consider someone you know (or have known) who is experiencing a mid-life reevaluation. Which of the five causes mentioned most apply to this individual?

3. Which of these six issues are (or have been) most difficult for you to face? Why?

4. Most people focus on the negative aspects of a mid-life reevaluation. Why can such a reevaluation be positive?

5. Name two significant life goals you have accomplished. Have those accomplishments satisfied or increased your thirst for "more"?

# CHAPTER THREE

## The Best Place to Be . . .
## Is Wherever You Are

Yesterday I had lunch with a church member who is experiencing a major crisis in his life. A decade ago he started a small computer store selling brand-name hardware and software at discount prices. He hit the market at just the right time and became one of those overnight successes you often read about. His new prosperity allowed him to do many of the things he had dreamed about. He purchased a winter home in New Mexico for frequent ski vacations. His children attended the best schools. He generously supported his local church and other Christian causes. He had it all—but he wanted more.

He was landlocked in his present location and could not build a bigger store. Not wanting to give up his profitable location, he decided to open another discount store on the other end of town.

His second store was not the overnight success his first one had been. By this time discount computer stores were no longer a novelty, and my friend was facing some stiff competition from national chains.

Then, he had a "brainstorm." Instead of having two stores, why not have eight? The economies of scale would allow him to saturate his community with advertising. Many of the fixed costs could be spread over eight locations easier than two. So my friend poured himself into opening six more outlets. The result? The continuing decline in computer prices, coupled with a downturn in the economy, forced my friend to close all of his stores. His one successful location had to be sold to erase the debt he had incurred from the other ventures.

He spent five years neglecting his family and other vital aspects of his life to expand a business that was already successful. In the end, he lost everything. All because he could not say "enough."

## ILLUSIONS AND DELUSIONS

Every man goes through a reevaluation period in his life—commonly known as a mid-life crisis. Such a period is not necessarily bad. It can lead to necessary course corrections in a man's life. But we benefit from these course corrections only if we have an accurate picture of where we are and where we are going.

On September 1, 1983, 269 innocent people lost their lives because of a navigational error by the pilots of Korean Airlines Flight 007. Reportedly, these pilots accidentally punched in the wrong set of navigational coordinates after a refueling stop in Alaska. From that point on, every new set of coordinates they entered sent them farther off track. As a result they unknowingly penetrated Soviet airspace, were attacked by a Soviet pilot, and plunged into the icy ocean below. The tragedy was a result of basing navigational decisions on wrong presuppositions.

In the same way, many of us today are making wrong choices involving our marriages, our investments, our jobs, and a number of other areas based on the illusion that happiness is over the next horizon. We have been deluded into thinking that somewhere out there is . . .

- a job that will utilize all of our gifts and interests and will provide maximum income with minimal effort.
- a "big deal" that will ensure financial security for the rest of our lives.
- a church that is completely free of any conflict and satisfies our every spiritual need.
- a friend who will always be there for us and will never ask anything in return.
- a period of time in our lives (known as retirement) when we will have lots of money and no responsibilities—except to entertain ourselves.
- a wife who has the body of Kim Basinger, the mind of Madam Curie, and the soul of Mother Theresa.

Let me say this to you as gently as I can. NONE OF THOSE THINGS ARE OUT THERE! They are mirages. The illusion of something better, and the delusion that we will can have it, cause many men to make serious navigational errors in their lives. The result? Not only is the man's life destroyed, but so are those "on board" with him. In his wonderful book *Point Man,* Steve Farrar uses this analogy:

> Sometimes life reminds me of flying a plane. Not just any plane, but a massive 747. My wife and I are up front in the cockpit. Right behind the cockpit door in first class are our three kids, one great-grandmother, two sets of grandparents, assorted uncles, aunts, cousins, nieces and nephews, and some close friends.
>
> As you go down the spiral staircase, you find all of the other people and things that travel with us through life. You'll find one church, two schools, three school teachers, a piano teacher, a pediatrician, a general practitioner, an allergist, a gynecologist, and an orthodontist,

an attorney trying to collect from the insurance company that won't pay the bills for my wife's whiplash, an accountant, a soccer team . . .

The way I figure it, most families have so much going on that they could easily fill up a 747 with everyone and everything that's a part of their lives.[1]

When a man gives up his marriage, his children, his job, or his financial sense in the quest for "something better," the results are just as serious as a 747 crashing into the ocean. Many innocent lives are destroyed. The secret to staying on course in life is the simple, but often misunderstood, word *contentment.*

## A MOST MISUNDERSTOOD WORD

When I talked with friends and family members about this book, I tried to explain it in simple terms: "The book shows men how to be content with the circumstances, choices, and even mistakes of their lives." It seemed that everyone I talked with had their own story to tell about some friend who: (a) ran off with his secretary, (b) lost all of his money, (c) blew his brains out, or (d) did all three because he was dissatisfied with life.

Everyone also raised an eyebrow and asked the same question, "How in the world are *you* going to write about contentment?" They went on to point out that I was a goal-oriented person, always pushing for something more. How could I, with a straight face, encourage people to be satisfied where they are? And who really wants to buy a book that tells you that some of the things you dream about are probably not going to happen?

Good questions, to be sure. But they arise from a basic misunderstanding of the word *contentment.* The word *content* is not a synonym for *lazy* or *sluggard* or *couch potato.* Instead, the word *contentment* comes from a word that means "containment." It refers to a person who is self-contained. He is able to derive satisfaction from his inner resources, rather than external sources. The person who is self-contained does not tie his emotional well-being to:

- the Dow Jones Industrial Average.
- a possible promotion.
- the outcome of next Sunday's game.
- his teenager's SAT score.
- the kind of automobile he is driving.

He understands that no matter what he achieves and acquires in life, it will never be enough. Instead, he looks inward for his happiness. Of course, for a Christian the inner resource that allows him to be happy, in spite of external circumstances, is his relationship with Jesus Christ.

The man who has learned contentment has not given up his goals. He has not resigned himself to settling for "second best." He realizes that there are many circumstances in his life over which he has no control. And that's all right with him. The man who has learned contentment believes that there is a sovereign God who is ultimately in control of his destiny. So what does it mean to be content?

*Contentment means being at peace with the unchange-able circumstances, choices, and even mistakes that shape our destiny.*

## THREE ENEMIES OF CONTENTMENT

Why do we have such a difficult time with contentment? There are several "enemies" of contentment:

### A Wrong Standard of Success

There are several popular measurements of success:

- the square footage of your home
- the number of employees you supervise
- the school your children attend
- your rank on your company's organizational report
- your salary
- your net worth

- the number of weeks you get for vacation
- your weight and percent of body fat

As popular as these standards are, none of them are biblical. I like Russ Crosson's definition of success in his book *A Life Well Spent:* "I am successful as I am in the process of being obedient and carefully doing all that God's Word says to do. For example, I am successful as I train and love my children (Eph. 6:4; Deut. 6:6–8) and love my wife (Eph. 5:28). These verses do not guarantee or promise financial blessings if I do what God's Word says. Rather, they free me up to realize that I can be successful whether or not I have money. Money is not the barometer."[2]

Crosson then goes on to define success as "the successful completion of right things." If you have been to any time management seminars, you have probably heard a lecture on priorities. The difference between a manager and a leader is this: a manager concentrates on "doing things right"; a leader, on the other hand, concentrates on "doing the *right* things." A salesman who spends hours filling out meticulous sales reports instead of moving the product is guilty of "doing things right" but not "doing the right things." The concept applies to all of life. As Jesus said, "For what will a man be profited, if he gains the whole world, and forfeits his soul?"(Matt. 16:26).

What are "the right things" to which we should devote ourselves? One is hard work. Colossians 3:23 tells us that "whatever you do, do your work heartily, as for the Lord rather than for men." As long as you work diligently at whatever job you have, you are a success in God's eyes—regardless of your income.

Another "right thing" to purse is harmonious relationships with your family and friends: "Do nothing from selfishness or empty conceit, but with humility of mind let each of you regard one another as more important than himself" (Phil. 2:3).

Finally, we should devote ourselves to raising godly children: "And these words, which I am commanding you today, shall be on your heart; and you shall teach them diligently to your sons and shall talk of them when you sit in your house and when you walk by the way and when you lie down and when you rise up" (Deut. 6:6–7).[3]

Let's stop for a moment and do a self-evaluation of each of these areas. On a scale of 1-5 (one being the lowest), how would you grade yourself in the following areas?

| | | | | | |
|---|---|---|---|---|---|
| I rarely "goof off" when I'm on the clock. | 1 | 2 | 3 | 4 | 5 |
| I rarely grumble about my job to other employees. | 1 | 2 | 3 | 4 | 5 |
| Excellence is a priority in my work. | 1 | 2 | 3 | 4 | 5 |
| I regularly tell my wife how much I love her. | 1 | 2 | 3 | 4 | 5 |
| I have done all I can to make peace with people I may have offended. | 1 | 2 | 3 | 4 | 5 |
| I have completely forgiven those who hurt me. | 1 | 2 | 3 | 4 | 5 |
| My children are a priority in my schedule. | 1 | 2 | 3 | 4 | 5 |
| I have several friends who unconditionally accept me. | 1 | 2 | 3 | 4 | 5 |
| I pray for my wife and children regularly. | 1 | 2 | 3 | 4 | 5 |
| My children know that their relationship with God is a priority with me. | 1 | 2 | 3 | 4 | 5 |
| My life is properly balanced. | 1 | 2 | 3 | 4 | 5 |

How you rate these statements probably reveals several insights. First, you are probably guilty of having some areas you need to improve. But you may also realize that if these things are the criteria of success, your life is in better shape than you thought! If we are going to enjoy contentment in our lives, we must begin to use the right standard to measure success.

## Unrealistic Expectations

I'm a sucker for success stories. I love the Horatio Alger rags-to-riches stories that remind us that in this great country of ours anybody can make it. Search the bookshelves of your local bookstore and you will discover a plethora of books that remind you to give up your small ambitions and you don't have to settle for second best. If you're in the mailroom today, there is no reason you can't be the CEO tomorrow. You may have only a high school diploma, but that shouldn't keep you from the White House some day. You may be one month away from foreclosure on your home, but there is a chance that tomorrow Ed McMahon might come knocking at your door with a ten-million-dollar check from American Family Publishers. Your son may be an average ball player today, but some day you might be cheering him on in the Super Bowl.

In Romans 12:3 Paul advises every man "not to think more highly of himself than he ought to think; but to think so as to have sound judgment."

## The "Oasis" Syndrome

Another enemy (closely related to unrealistic expectations) that robs us of contentment is the belief that there must be something better than what we are experiencing now. Some years ago a network documentary entitled "But What If the Dream Comes True?" vividly demonstrated the "oasis" syndrome through the life of a forty-one-year-old man named Sam Greenwalt. Sam had worked hard all of his life to reach the vice-presidency of a bank. He and his family lived in the fashionable Detroit suburb of Birmingham. Were they happy there? Hardly. They were planning a move to an even more affluent suburb. Sam confessed, "It's like the camel driver going to the next oasis."

The documentary concluded with this observation: "The American dream grants you your wishes, and then cuts you into pieces. You struggle to reach Birmingham, but once there, you find life fragmented, family life threatened, the pressures as high as the taxes. So you look for an even bigger house in an even better neighborhood. . . . The new house is the new dream."[4]

I have often wondered why we are so prone to fall for the "oasis" syndrome. We know intellectually that Shangri-La does not exist. There is no perfect job, no adequate income, no flawless wife, no conflict-free church. But we keep searching. Why? To quit searching for these things would force us to look inside ourselves for our emotional well-being. And while we men may not be in regular contact with our souls, most of us know that our internal reservoir of resources are not adequate to supply our deepest needs. So we keep searching until we have exhausted every possible avenue of happiness and, like Solomon, conclude, "Meaningless! Meaningless! . . . Everything is meaningless" (Eccl. 1:2, NIV).

The goal of *The Road Most Traveled* is to help you stop the futile search for the oasis before you waste any more time and energy. How can you learn to be at peace with the unavoidable circumstances, choices, and even mistakes of your life?

In Philippians 4:11–12 Paul writes, "For I have learned to be content in whatever circumstance I am. I know how to get along with humble means, and I also know how to live in prosperity; in any and every circumstance I have learned the secret of being filled and going hungry, both of having abundance and suffering need." Remember where Paul was when he wrote these words? He wasn't on the French Riviera sipping a cold drink. Instead, he was in a Roman prison facing the threat of execution. Paul's natural response should have been panic. Yet Paul was able to say he had learned how to be content—how to be at peace—with his present circumstances. How?

## PAUL'S SECRETS OF CONTENTMENT

Paul had discovered three basic principles about contentment.

### A Life that Is Ministry-Focused

Paul had one passion in life: to spread the gospel of Jesus Christ to as many people as possible. That had not always been true. There was a time when he was obsessed with acquiring the most advanced educational degrees, driving the latest-model chariot, wearing designer tunics, and persecuting Christians.

But his face-to-face confrontation with Jesus Christ changed all of that. "But whatever things were gain to me, those things I have counted as loss for the sake of Christ. More than that, I count all things to be loss in view of the surpassing value of knowing Christ Jesus my Lord, for whom I have suffered the loss of all things, and count them but rubbish in order that I may gain Christ" (Phil. 3:7–8).

Paul's focus on ministry gave him a different filter through which to view his circumstances. Had his goal in life been peace and prosperity, then being in a Roman prison would have been a great catastrophe. But notice how Paul's ministry focus changed his perspective: "Now I want you to know, brethren, that my circumstances have turned out for the greater progress of the gospel, so that my imprisonment in the cause of Christ has become well known throughout the whole praetorian guard and to everyone else, and that most of the brethren, trusting in the Lord because of my imprisonment, have far more courage to speak the word of God without fear" (Phil. 1:12–14).

Paul's ministry perspective allowed him to see real benefits from his imprisonment. First, the guards to whom he was chained were hearing the gospel. In fact, Paul says the gospel was spreading throughout the entire imperial guard unit. Also, other believers were gaining boldness in their witness for Christ because of Paul's situation. Paul was happy to give up everything—even his own life—if it resulted in the realization of his life purpose.

What is the overriding passion in your life? If your answer involves a position in the corporation, an investment portfolio, a relationship, or a particular lifestyle, then any adversities you face are problems. Financial problems, the death of loved ones, illnesses, the loss of a job, are all detours to your goals.

But if your life goal is bigger than yourself and is centered around spreading the gospel of Christ, then all of those problems can actually be ministry opportunities in disguise. Someone has written:

If for me to live is money, then to die is to leave it all behind.

If for me to live is fame, then to die is to be quickly forgotten.

If for me to live is power and influence, then to die is to lose both.

If for me to live is possessions, then to die is to depart with nothing in my hands.

But if for me to live is Christ, then to die is gain.[5]

Paul's first secret of contentment was learning to be ministry-focused rather than self-focused.

### Express Gratitude to God

Last year my grandfather died. Next to my parents, he was my greatest encourager in life. About five years before his death, he suffered a tragedy that few men could bear to endure. His wife of fifty years became desperately ill. Then, six months later my mother (his only daughter) developed colon cancer. Within a six-week period both his wife and his daughter died. Although he was overcome with grief, he never once blamed God. Instead, he always thanked the Lord for the fifty-eight years he had with my grandmother, and the fifty-five years he had with my mother. When we would visit him those last years of his life, we would take him to the cemetery where his two "angels" were buried. He would have my uncle, my brother, my sister, and me join hands together to pray and then to sing this song:

When upon life's billows you are tempest tossed,
When you are discouraged, thinking all is lost,
Count your many blessings, name them one by one,
And it will surprise you what the Lord hath done.
Count your blessings, name them one by one.
Count your blessings, see what God hath done;
Count your blessings, name them one by one;
Count your many blessings, see what God hath done.[6]

My grandfather understood that one important secret to

accepting life's circumstances is to thank God for what He has given us, rather than blame God for what He hasn't given us.

In Paul's letter to the Philippians, he mentions rejoicing—expressing gratitude to God—nineteen times. "Rejoice in the Lord always; again I will say, rejoice!" (Phil. 4:4). Both my grandfather and Paul understood that it is impossible for discontent and gratitude to exist in the same heart.

## Trust in the Sovereignty of God

Paul was convinced that his circumstances were orchestrated by a sovereign God. The apostle did not know whether imprisonment would result in his death or not. But he was content to leave the final outcome in God's hands: "For I know that this shall turn out for my deliverance through your prayers and the provision of the Spirit of Jesus Christ" (Phil. 1:19). Whether his "deliverance" would be from prison or from this earth, Paul trusted in God's plan for his life.

Do you believe in a sovereign God who is in control of every part of your life? Without thinking, most people would answer, "Of course I believe in a sovereign God. Who doesn't?" But think for a moment what that means. If God is truly sovereign, then God has either planned or allowed *every* circumstance in your life. "Every" includes cancer, divorce, the death of a loved one, severed friendships, and the loss of a job. Do you still believe in the sovereignty of God? If you are having a difficult time swallowing this idea (and most of us do at one time or another), just look at what the Bible teaches about God's control over our circumstances:

> The mind of man plans his way, but the LORD directs his steps. (Prov. 16:9)
>
> Many are the plans in a man's heart, but it is the LORD's purpose that prevails. (Prov. 19:21, NIV)
>
> Thine eyes have seen my unformed substance; and in Thy book they were all written, the days that were ordained for me, when as yet there was not one of them. (Ps. 139:16)

"Can I not, O house of Israel, deal with you as this potter does?" declares the LORD. "Behold, like the clay in the potter's hand, so are you in My hand, O house of Israel." (Jer. 18:6)

It is always amazing to me the number of people—even Christians—who react negatively to the truth of God's sovereign control over our lives. I remember preaching a sermon on the subject of God's sovereignty in one of my former churches. The next day I heard through the grapevine that a handful of deacons were upset about my message and were planning to ambush me at our Tuesday night deacon's meeting. Sure enough, when the chairman called for "other business" (always a tense moment for most pastors), the attack began. "You and I must serve a different God." "If God has planned every part of my life, doesn't that just make us a bunch of robots?" "How can evil be a part of God's plan when the Bible says God hates evil."

Fortunately, I had arranged for enough Bibles in the meeting room so that everyone could have his own copy. Knowing that I was going to be challenged that evening, I duplicated a list of all the Bible verses I could find about God's sovereignty. For the next forty-five minutes we simply turned to those verses and read them one after another. By the time we were finished, most of the deacons saw that the sovereignty of God is not only a biblical doctrine, it is a comforting one. How reassuring it is to know that Someone wiser and more powerful than we is directing our lives.

The rest of this book is dedicated to helping you trust in God's sovereignty over every aspect of your life: your circumstances, your choices, and yes, even your mistakes. When we understand God's design and control over every aspect of our life, we can experience real contentment. An "ordinary" life becomes "extraordinary" when we realize the uniqueness of God's plan for us.

The first life area we are going to examine is perhaps the most difficult for men to experience contentment. But I believe it is the most basic.

## FOR FURTHER REFLECTION

1. In several sentences, describe your idea of a "perfect" life. Be honest.

2. How does the author define *contentment?* Why is this word so often misunderstood?

3. Paraphrase the author's definition of *success.* According to this definition are you more or less successful than you thought? Why?

4. Which of the "enemies of contentment" most applies to your life situation? Why?

5. How would you answer the question, "What is the overriding passion of your life?" What is the relationship between your answer to this question and your level of contentment?

# CHAPTER FOUR

## Seeing God's Hand in Your Finances

This summer Amy and I will have been married twenty years. It is hard for me to believe that the little girl I met in math class in the seventh grade has been my best friend and companion for almost thirty years. We have been discussing how to best celebrate this milestone. Our plans now are to spend a week in Maui—the site of our honeymoon. I don't remember a lot of the details of that week on the islands (I imagine I was still in shock over the wedding), but I do remember the feeling I had as we landed at the DFW airport one hot August morning and drove to our apartment in a run-down area close to downtown Dallas, Texas, where I was about to enter the seminary.

There is no place more miserable than Dallas in August. I longed to be back on the beaches of Hawaii enjoying the cool ocean breeze and the carefree existence of the island. I immediately began plotting how Amy and I could return within the next two years. I calculated that if we could save $60 a month for two years, we could probably swing it. Such a task would not be easy. I would be in school and Amy would be earning $600 a month as a teacher, but it would be worth the sacrifice.

During that first week of August 1977, it would have been hard for me to conceive that I would be where I am now financially. (I'm sure the same thing is true for most of you as you look back twenty years.) But it would have been even harder to have believed that I would not be content with my present financial status.

When we married, Amy was earning $7,200 a year. We were able to make it just fine on her salary and even save a little bit for that Hawaiian vacation. After our first year of marriage, I was hired as a youth minister in a large downtown church. I was flabbergasted to learn the salary I would receive—$9,600 a year. How in the world could two people *ever* hope to spend that much money? Yet our income today does not seem to be enough.

Many people measure their financial status by the automobile they drive. During those early days of our marriage I drove a yellow Volkswagen Bug with a black racing stripe down the center. The front right seat had been ripped out, so that any passenger had to sit in the back seat.

One week Amy and I house-sat for a couple in our church. They gave me permission to drive their car—a big blue Buick. As long as I live I will never forget the sensation of driving that car, with the air conditioner running full blast and listening to an eight-track tape of The Carpenters (remember, this was the 70s). I vowed to myself that one day I would own such an automobile.

Today, the church I serve provides me with a car. You guessed it—a big blue Buick, complete with stereo cassette player. Don't misunderstand, I love the car and am grateful for it. But part of my Saturday morning ritual is turning to the automobile section of the paper and salivating over a car that better suits me. A big white Lincoln Town Car would do nicely, thank you.

## NEVER ENOUGH CAN BE TOO MUCH

Believing God is in control of our lives includes believing He's in charge of our financial picture. Yet, one of the most difficult areas for us to experience contentment is with our finances. No matter how much we have, we will always want more. Being at peace with your economic circumstances is the foundation for contentment in most other life areas. Why, then, do so many of us feel like we don't have enough?

### Not Understanding the Limits of Money

King Solomon knew about the limitations of money:

Whoever loves money never has money enough;
    whoever loves wealth is never satisfied with his income.
    This too is meaningless.

As goods increase,
    so do those who consume them.
And what benefit are they to the owner
    except to feast his eyes on them?

The sleep of a laborer is sweet,
    whether he eats little or much,
but the abundance of a rich man
    permits him no sleep.

I have seen a grievous evil under the sun:

wealth hoarded to the harm of its owner,
    or wealth lost through some misfortune. . . .
Naked a man comes from his mother's womb,
    and as he comes, so he departs.
He takes nothing from his labor
    that he can carry in his hand.

                 (Eccl. 5:10–15, NIV)

Solomon understood the limits of money as well as anyone. The richest man of his day, he discovered the truth that money cannot satisfy. As he looked back over his personal experience, the wise king reminds us of five limitations of money.

*You can never have enough money.* "Whoever loves money never has money enough; whoever loves wealth is never satisfied with his income." We've all experienced that. The raise you so desperately wanted last year comes and then is quickly forgotten as you anticipate what you will earn next year. I counsel with couples all the time who lament, "We are making more money than we have ever made before, but where does it all go?" Solomon answers that question by observing that "As goods increase, so do those who consume them." That is, the higher the income, the greater your expenses.

I thought about these words last week as I talked with my sister and brother-in-law, a pastor in Tyler, Texas. Recently a larger church contacted them about coming to serve their congregation. I was surprised that they had no interest in making the move. They were content with their church, their home, and their salary. "You realize that you probably would make at least $20,000 more a year," I reasoned. My sister pointed out that even if their income rose, their expenses would too. They would need to relocate to another home and pay a higher interest rate than they were paying now. They would be expected to dress in a way befitting their new position—that costs money. They would pay more in taxes. The increased demands on my brother-in-law's time would force him to pay for services he had been performing himself, like mowing the lawn or servicing his car.

The net financial benefit of moving would be far less than I had calculated. Why? Because "as goods increase, so do those who consume them."

*Money causes anxiety.* Solomon says that the common laborer sleeps peacefully, but the wealth of the rich man "permits him no sleep." A janitor or clerk punches in at 8:00 and punches out at 5:00. He goes home and showers, eats supper, plays with the kids and sits down in front of the tube to watch his favorite show. He doesn't think about his job until he punches in the next morning.

However, the manager's job does not end at 5:00. He is constantly worrying about sales figures, the payroll, corporate politics, and endless government regulations. He is also concerned with preserving and increasing his own investment portfolio. Who is enjoying life? Increased wealth exacts a cost.

*Money can be harmful.* If you are not careful, money can rob you of happiness both in this life and in the life to come. Solomon had observed people who had hoarded money "to the harm of its owner." There is a difference between *saving* money and *hoarding* money. Solomon extols the value of saving money. "Go to the ant, O sluggard, observe her ways and be wise, which, having no chief, officer or ruler, prepares her food in the summer, and gathers her provision in the harvest" (Prov. 6:6–8). We should systematically set aside some of our income for future or unexpected needs.

But hoarding money is stockpiling cash for no other reason than seeing how big a pile you can stash away. For some, it is a game. For others, money becomes a god to whom they look for protection from the adversities and uncertainties of life. Whatever the motivation, Solomon says that hoarding money is harmful.

One couple I know worked and saved all of their lives and had accumulated a net worth of more than a million dollars. Through their fifty years of marriage they had dreamed of taking an around-the-world luxury cruise. Yet they never felt like they had quite enough money to justify such an expenditure. Finally, they decided to bite the bullet and take the trip. However, a few months before they were scheduled to sail, the wife suddenly died of a heart attack. The husband was left with his pile of money, an additional $500,000 life insurance policy from his wife, and a lot of regrets. When I visited with him in his home after the funeral, he was holding the travel brochure in his hands and lamenting, "If only we had taken that trip." That is what Solomon means by "wealth hoarded to the harm of its owner."

*Money is easily lost.* Last year an editor for a Sunday School curriculum series called me and asked me if I would be interested in a writing assignment. I already had a book project that would soon be due, along with plenty of projects around the church. But I figured that I could give up some time on Saturday for a few months, and I could earn about $3,000. I rationalized that I could spend this extra money on my family—maybe a nice vacation in the summer. Several weeks into the assignment, a friend called and invited me to participate in an investment deal. The cost? $3,500. I agreed to participate since I was going to have an additional $3,000 in a few months from my writing assignment. Within a few weeks the deal went sour and I lost all $3,500. I spent the next three months sacrificing my day off in order to make money, not to spend on my family, but to pay for funds I had lost.

Solomon must have had his share of "wealth lost through some misfortune." It is ridiculous to build your life around a commodity like money that is so easily lost. No matter how much money you earn or save, it can be wiped out in an instant—through a poor investment, an accident, or a lawsuit. That is why Solomon urged us to strive for balance in our lives. "Do not wear yourself out to get rich; have the wisdom to show restraint. Cast but a glance at riches, and they are gone, for they will surely sprout wings and fly off to the sky like an eagle" (Prov. 23:4–5, NIV).

*Money is only temporal.* Perhaps the greatest limitation of money is that you will leave every cent you earn behind. You've no doubt heard the old saying, "You can't take it with you." Solomon expresses that maxim more eloquently. "Naked a man comes from his mother's womb, and as he comes, so he departs. He takes nothing from his labor that he can carry in his hand."

I couldn't help but laugh at the following letter that appeared in Ann Lander's column:

> Aunt "Emma" was married to a tightwad who was also a little strange. He made a good salary, but they lived frugally because he insisted on putting 20 percent of his

paycheck under the mattress. . . . The money, he said, was going to come in handy in their old age.

When Uncle "Ollie" was sixty, he was stricken with cancer. Toward the end, he made Aunt Emma promise, in the presence of his brothers, that she would put the money he had stashed away in his coffin so he could buy his way into heaven if he had to. They all knew he was a little odd, but this was clearly a crazy request. Aunt Em did promise, however, and assured Uncle Ollie's brothers that she was a woman of her word and would do as he asked.

The following morning she took the money (about $26,000) to the bank and deposited it. She then wrote a check and put in the coffin four days later.[1]

I think about my own father. For thirty years he labored at a job he hated in order to support our family. He prided himself on his ability to accumulate a large amount of money from a modest salary.

Then one day he went to the doctor for a routine checkup. Just two words from the doctor changed his life: pancreatic cancer. He was given three months to live (he lasted four) and sent home to die. One day during the last weeks of his life' he sat down with me to review the locations of his varied investments—accumulated money representing years of sacrifice and self-denial. He looked at me, his oldest son, smiled, and observed, "Isn't it ironic? I've worked all of my life for money and now I am going to have to leave it to someone else."[2]

Quit mortgaging your life for something you will ultimately leave behind. Instead of lamenting over money you don't have, enjoy the income you *do* have.

## Comparing Our Financial Status to Others

Another enemy of contentment is comparison. We love to compare ourselves to other people. That is especially true about men and their money. Dr. Lee Salk, a professor of psychology at Cornell Medical Center writes, "People jockey to find out what other people earn because, in our society, money is a symbol of strength, influence, and power."[3]

Consider the following chart from the U.S. Census Bureau showing average household income:

| Income | % of Households |
|---|---|
| $14,999 or less | 23.4 |
| $15,000–$24,999 | 16.9 |
| $25,000–$34,999 | 14.7 |
| $35,000–$49,999 | 16.3 |
| $50,000–$74,999 | 16.1 |
| $75,000–$99,999 | 6.7 |
| $100,000 or more | 5.8[4] |

Which part of the graph first caught your attention: the percent of people earning more than you, or the percent of people earning less than you? Most people I know focus on the group earning more. That's human nature. We tend to judge how we are doing by the economic standards of those who are better off than we are. We forget that there are many people who are exactly where we are, or maybe even worse off. By the way, did you notice the fact that if your household income (that means all gross salaries, interest and dividend income, pension payments, rents received, etc.) is $50,000 or more, you are better off than 88 percent of the country? One of the problems with comparison is that it causes us to focus on what we don't have, instead of what we have already.

Comparison also causes us to forget God's unique plan for our lives. God's sovereign purpose extends to every aspect of our existence: our physical appearance, our emotional makeup, our jobs, our spouses, and, yes, even our financial status. That is why comparison is such a potent deterrent to contentment. Oscar Wilde illustrated how Satan can use comparison to rob us of contentment:

> The devil was once crossing the Libyan desert, and he came upon a spot where a number of small fiends were tormenting a holy hermit. The sainted man easily shook off their evil suggestions. The devil watched their failure, and then he stepped forward to give them a lesson. "What you do is too crude," he said. "Permit me for one moment." With that he whispered to the holy man, "Your brother has just been made Bishop of Alexandria." A scowl of malignant jealousy at once clouded the serene face of the hermit. "That," said the devil to his imps, "is the sort of thing which I should recommend."[5]

### A Consumptive Vs. Ministry Lifestyle

My friend Bobb Biehl says that every life exists for one of two purposes: to meet a need or to feed a greed. Bobb is simply saying that every person's life is either focused on self or on service. If your life is centered around self-gratification, I can promise you two things. First, you will never be satisfied. Our old friend Solomon talked about the futility of pleasure. Second, you will waste *a lot* of money in your search for meaning. You will try new cars, new homes, new wardrobes, new hobbies, and maybe even new wives, but will still come up empty.

On the other hand, if your life is centered around finding and fulfilling God's unique purpose for your life, your economic status will become secondary. Like Paul, you will be able to rejoice in whatever circumstance you find yourself.

Gordon MacDonald tells the true story of a black pastor in South Africa whose home was fire-bombed and destroyed one night. The next morning the minister and his family stood out in front of their burned-out home. All that was left was the chimney. Personal belongings, furniture, books, and sermon notes had been reduced to a heap of ashes. A visitor to the scene noticed that the pastor had taken a lump of charcoal and written some words on the chimney wall—words the visitor recognized as the vow taken by all Methodist pastors each year at the District Conference:

> Put me to what you will,
> Put me to doing,
> Put me to suffering,
> Let me be laid aside for you,
> Let me have all things,
> Let me have nothing.
> I freely and heartily yield
> All things to your pleasure and disposal.[6]

What is your life purpose? Why do you think God placed you on this planet? What unique contribution can you make to the kingdom of God? When those questions become the focus of your life, you will automatically become more content with your financial status. Why? A life purpose built around service, rather than self, results in a diminishing interest in material expenditures.

## FOUR STEPS TO EXPERIENCING CONTENTMENT WITH YOUR FINANCES

How can you experience contentment with your finances? Let me share with you several important principles that have helped me and those with whom I have counseled.

### Calculate Your True Net Worth

Do you know how much you are really worth? Most people don't. They have a vague idea what they have in the bank or with a broker. They look at their retirement accounts once a year. They have attached an approximate value to their homes. But they have never added all of those figures together. Let me encourage you to take a few minutes to fill out the following net worth statement:

## LIST OF FINANCIAL ASSETS

LIQUID ASSETS

| | |
|---|---|
| Cash on hand and checking accounts | $ _____ |
| Money market funds | _____ |
| CDs | _____ |
| Savings accounts | _____ |
| Bonds | _____ |
| Stocks | _____ |
| Life insurance (cash value) | _____ |
| Other _____ | _____ |
| _____ | _____ |
| _____ | _____ |
| Total liquid assets | $ _____ |

NON-LIQUID ASSETS

| | |
|---|---|
| Home (less mortgage) | $ _____ |
| Other real estate (less mortgage) | _____ |
| Limited partnerships | _____ |
| Cars | _____ |
| Personal property | _____ |
| Furniture | _____ |
| IRAs | _____ |
| Pensions and/or 401k plans | _____ |
| Notes receivable | _____ |
| Other _____ | _____ |
| _____ | _____ |
| _____ | _____ |
| Total non-liquid assets | $ _____ |
| TOTAL ASSETS (liquid and non-liquid) | $ _____ |

Did you discover that you are worth more than you thought? One secret of learning to become content with our finances is to thank God for what He has *already* given us.

### Determine Your Monthly and Your Yearly "Nut"

Those of you who live on commission income or run your own business understand the concept of "the nut." Your monthly "nut" refers to the minimum amount of money you need each month to meet your essential expenses: house payment or rent, utilities, food, and so on. Why is this figure important to calculate? Obviously, you need to know how much income you need to meet your obligations. If your monthly "nut" is $5,000 and your income is $3,000, you have a $2,000 problem.

This exercise can also promote contentment with your present financial situation. One way to combat the insatiable desire for more is to determine what your income needs *really* are. How *little* could you get by on each month? I'll guarantee it is less than you think.

Last night I listened to a woman on the radio tell how she and her family of six lived amazingly well on an income of $25,000. In fact, for the last several years she has been publishing a monthly newsletter called *The Tightwad's Gazette* that has more than 50,000 subscribers who want to learn how to get by on less. As I listened to this woman and thought about my family's situation, I realized that we could live on a lot less income if we had to. It might not be much fun, but we could survive. Calculating my monthly and yearly "nut" made me extremely grateful for the income that God has given me.

One secret of the apostle Paul's contentment in life was that he was not paralyzed with fear about his finances. He realized that his financial situation could change in an instant. He was emotionally prepared for every contingency. "For I have learned to be content in whatever circumstances I am. I know how to get along with humble means, and I also know how to live in prosperity; in any and every circumstance I have learned the secret of being filled and going hungry, both of having abundance and suffering need" (Phil. 4:11–12).

## Eliminate "Window Shopping" from Your Schedule

At the risk of losing my credibility as a member of the male gender, let me make a painful confession: I *like* to go to the mall (let me quickly add, however, *not* with my wife). Sometimes on my day off I will drive to Dallas and spend hours roaming around a shopping center. I have several favorite stops. One is a fashionable men's shoe store featuring hand-crafted leather and alligator shoes. Another is an upscale department store that carries some of the finest suits available. I also have a favorite place to browse for neckties. After several hours of "shopping" I sit down at a coffee bar in the middle of the mall and dream about the thrill of purchasing those items when I finally "make it."

The truth is I have more shoes, suits, and ties than a man could possibly want or need. Amy jokes that my closet looks like a men's store. But "enough" is never enough. My days spent window shopping only fuel my desire for more. I am not alone. According to recent statistics, about 70 percent of all adults visit a regional mall weekly. The number of malls has grown from 2,000 in 1957 to more than 30,000 today. According to a survey of 34,300 mall shoppers, only 25 percent said that they had come in pursuit of a specific item. The rest were there to "browse."[8]

Maybe you are like most men who would rather endure bamboo shoots under your toenails than spend your day off at the mall. But are there habits you have that increase your level of discontent? Like flipping through the latest issue of *Golf Digest* and salivating over that new set of clubs. Or making an annual pilgrimage to the boat show to view the latest products. How about spending a Saturday morning at the car dealership checking out the latest vehicles? I am not suggesting any of these activities is wrong. Yet we need to recognize that they are many times counterproductive to developing the attitude of contentment.

## Hold Your Money Loosely

Corrie ten Boom, that great woman of God immortalized in the book *The Hiding Place,* once said, "I have learned to hold those things dearest to me loosely in my hands. That way it does not hurt as much when God pries them from my fingers." I have discovered that the best way to be content with my finances is to realize that none of it really belongs to me anyway. The more loosely I hold my money, the more likely I am to be content with my financial condition. If my hand is completely open anyway, what difference does it make how much I am holding?

How do you hold your money "loosely"? By regularly giving it away—to your church, to other evangelical causes, to your children, and to those less fortunate than yourself. There is something about regularly letting go of our money that liberates us from concern about our finances. Several years ago I read a book that addressed letting go of money. The book issued a challenge to identify someone less fortunate than yourself and give him a large sum of money. I immediately thought of a custodian in our church who was struggling financially. God brought to my mind the sum of $1,000 to give him. But the more I thought about giving away that money, the more uncomfortable I became. I went through every logical and illogical rationalization you can imagine:

- "What if I gave everyone in need a thousand dollars? I would be destitute!"
- "What if God is trying to discipline this man through his financial need and I interfere?"
- "What if I suddenly die and my family needs this money?"
- "What if I just keep the money and invest it wisely? Maybe I will have more to give later!"

The fact that I was having such a difficult time giving the money away confirmed how much I really needed to. (And yes, I finally did give him the money.) John Wesley once said, "If you have any desire to escape the damnation of hell, give all you can; otherwise I can have no more hope of your salvation than that of Judas Iscariot."[9] While Wesley was using hyperbole, we should not miss the truth of his statement. Jesus said it clearly: "'No one can serve two masters; for either he will hate the one and love the other, or he will *hold to one* [emphasis mine] and despise the other. You cannot serve God and mammon [money]" (Matt. 6:24). Period.

How loosely are you holding your money? Are you able to give it away freely to others? Are you investing your money in ways that will make an eternal impact? In his book *The Challenge of a Disciplined Life,* Richard Foster writes, "Suppose that the United States decided to change over its entire currency to British pounds, that the moment it did all American currency would be worthless, but that we were not told when the monetary conversion would take place. In that situation, the wise course would be to turn our money into British pounds, keeping only enough American currency to live day to day."[10]

What a great analogy to eternity! Do you realize that one day, every dollar you have accumulated is going to suddenly become worthless? The Bible says, "Riches do not profit in the day of wrath" (Prov. 11:4). That means that every dollar, share of stock, certificate of deposit, bond, and 401k account will be declared "void" when Jesus Christ returns to judge the world.

Knowing that, what should be our attitude about money? Contrary to popular thinking, the Bible does not condemn money. Jesus affirms that money can have eternal value if used properly. It is often said, "You can't take it with you." That's true. But you can send it ahead of you by investing in God's kingdom. Consider the words of Jesus:

> "Do not lay up for yourselves treasures upon earth, where moth and rust destroy, and where thieves break in and steal. But lay up for yourselves treasures in heaven, where neither moth nor rust destroys, and where thieves do not break in or steal; for where your treasure is, there will your heart be also." (Matt. 6:19–21)
>
> "And I say to you, make friends for yourselves by means of the mammon [money] of unrighteousness; that when it fails, they may receive you into the eternal dwellings. He who is faithful in a very little thing is faithful

also in much; and he who is unrighteous in a very little
thing is unrighteous also in much." (Luke 16:9–10)

How many people will be in heaven one day to welcome you
because of the financial investment you have made in God's
kingdom?

Whether you have a few hundred or a few million is not the
real issue about your money. The Bible teaches that God takes a
large part of the responsibility for our financial condition: "[He]
shows no partiality to princes, nor regards the rich above the
poor, for they *all are the work of His hands* [emphasis mine]"
(Job 34:19). The bottom-line issue regarding money is how you
use what you have. Some of your money should be used for your
and your family's enjoyment. Some should be saved for future
needs. Jesus reminds us that some money should be invested in
those things that will live on after we die.

Are you grateful for what God has already given you? Why not
take a moment right now to thank your heavenly Father for His
material blessings in your life?

Contentment with our finances is almost inseparably linked
to another life area that is the focus of our next chapter.

## FOR FURTHER REFLECTION

1. How does your financial condition now compare to ten years ago? Twenty years ago? Compare your lifestyle to that of your parents at your age. What causes you to want more?

2. What fuels discontent in our culture? Can you lessen the impact of those cultural factors in your life? How?

3. How can the accumulation of money harm people in this life? What about in eternity?

4. Describe the relationship between one's life purpose and his contentment with his financial condition.

5. If your family income were suddenly cut in half, how long would you be able to survive? What steps should you take now to ensure that you could survive in that situation?

# CHAPTER FIVE

## Seeing God's Hand in Your Work

The great Russian novelist Fyodor Dostoyevsky once said that if you truly wanted to destroy a man, just give him work that was of a completely senseless, irrational nature. He believed that if people were deprived of meaningful work, they would lose their purpose for living and go stark, raving mad.[1] If that is true, then we had better start building more insane asylums. Why? According to Paul Goodman, author of *Growing Up Absurd,* more than 70 percent of all American workers get little or no gratification out of their jobs. And lest you think that these seventy percent are mostly factory workers performing monotonous tasks, Goodman quickly adds that only 10 percent of those 70 percent work on an assembly line.

Regardless of economic status, the majority of us are finding little enjoyment from our work, which is tragic considering the fact that our jobs account for almost 60 percent of our lives. Gordon MacDonald, in *Living at High Noon,* recounts the experience of sitting next to a well-known television star on a transatlantic flight:

> For almost five hours we talked about some of the salient issues of life. My traveling partner had no hesitation in admitting that he was a bored, unhappy man, feeling betrayed that success had brought him so little of that feeling of excitement he'd expected when he'd started. Looking back on our conversation, I now realize that at mid-life he was still tyrannized by the thought that, given enough success, his job would become one long orgy of excitement and satisfaction. I remember saying to him, "You know, you already have the three things the average American male thinks epitomizes vocational success: a beautiful young wife, more money from your work than you could ever spend, and a name so popular that in two lifetimes you can't handle all the invitations you get." The memory of what my friend said on the plane has stuck with me. "You're right; I've got all that. But it's those very things that have conspired to make me generally miserable. For you see now that I have achieved them, I know—unlike those still reaching for them—that they're not worth having, not worth working as hard for as I've done."[2]

## HOW WE FEEL ABOUT WHAT WE DO

Whether our job is on the assembly line, in the manager's chair, or in front of the television camera, most of us *endure* rather than *enjoy* our work. Our negative feeling toward work is especially acute during the mid-life reevaluation. A friend of mine who is a management consultant says that the average age most men begin their own business is thirty-nine. Is that really surprising? Sometime between the ages of thirty-five and forty-five, men begin to ask themselves some very serious questions about their vocation:

- Is this really what I want to spend the rest of my life doing?
- Why haven't I gone further in my career?
- Is this job worth mortgaging my health and/or my family?
- Could I find another job if I were laid off?
- What eternal difference am I making through my job?

Why are we more prone to ask these questions between the ages of thirty-five and forty-five? Actually, all of us *should* reevaluate our jobs from time to time. Have you ever been driving and had this funny feeling that you were lost? Not wanting to admit your mistake, you keep going in the wrong direction hoping that everything will turn out all right. The longer you go, the more difficult it is to admit that you have made a mistake. In the same way, an honest evaluation of your job may lead you to abandon a career that once suited you, but no longer meets your financial and/or emotional needs.

## TIME TO REEVALUATE

Not long ago I read a book by a prominent minister who suddenly abandoned his spectacular career. Many in his denomination were shocked at his sudden action. Why would anyone trade a prestigious position for a job paying a third of what he had been making? Many people speculated that there had to be some dark, hidden secret at the bottom of his decision. No one in their right mind would make such a choice. Or would they? In his own words, the minister reveals that his decision was anything but "sudden." In fact, he had thought of leaving the ministry before:

> Not long after returning from Korea, I kept a speaking engagement in Boston. . . . I walked around Boston Common in a detached frame of mind. . . . At the same

time, the national law school fair met in a nearby exhibition building. I spent hours talking to the representatives of major and minor law schools. After purchasing a kit on learning to take the LSAT, I began to consider a radical change in direction altogether. As the jet rolled out at Boston's Logan International, I was taking sample LSAT tests. After twenty-five years in ministry, three degrees, six churches, and thousands of sermons, I was on the brink of chunking it to be a lawyer.[3]

When did this minister make his radical vocational change? You guessed it. In the mid-life years. This minister's case is not unique. I believe that most men during their mid-life years seriously consider the possibility of a different career. What is it about this period that causes us to do some serious reevaluation of our lives?

## The Changing Values Syndrome

In their early adult years, most men are singularly focused on advancing in their career and accumulating capital. I believe that they don't consciously want to neglect their family or their spiritual lives, but they have the feeling that those things can wait. "After all, I have an entire lifetime to build a relationship with my family. The best thing I can do for them is to provide for their financial needs."

But sometime during the mid-life period, we begin to realize that time is passing more quickly than we thought. Our toddlers are now in their preteen years. Our wives may have experienced a close call with cancer. We realize that we have more years behind us than in front of us. And suddenly, the things that we took for granted in our early adult years become more valuable to us.

These realizations give men a completely different perspective about their jobs. No longer are they thrilled about out-of-town travel or high-energy meetings that last through dinner time. Instead, these things are seen as intrusions to "what really matters." This definite shift in values causes a man to reassess his career. The man in this period of reevaluation asks himself, "What does it profit a man if he gain the whole world, but loses his soul (or family, or health)?"

## The Glass Ceiling Syndrome

Another reason men reevaluate their job in the mid-life years is what I call "the glass ceiling" syndrome. This is the realization that you have gone about as far in your career as you are going to go. The vocational dreams you had as a young adult are not going to be realized: You will never be the president of the company. You will never be the pastor of a megachurch. You will never be superintendent of the school district.

In fact, the only chance you have to reach the upper levels of your vocation is to *change* vocations. The mid-life years offer your last opportunity to do so. Daniel Levinson, the mid-life expert, clearly explains this phenomenon:

> Often, a man who has worked hard during his 30's comes to recognize in the midlife transition that his accumulated achievements and skills do not provide a basis for further advancement. He cannot become a writer, educator, political leader, or violin maker of the caliber he imagined. He will never rise to the level he sought in the military, the corporation, or the church. He will fall short of his early dream. This is a crucial turning point. He may decide to continue in his present job, doing work that is increasingly routine and humiliating. He may change to another job or another occupation, that offers more challenge and satisfaction or he may reduce his interest in work, performing well enough to keep employed by investing himself in other aspects of life such as family or leisure.[4]

Notice that Levinson says that one option for the man who has hit the glass ceiling is to change careers. "If I am never going to be the president of the company, why not cash in my retirement and do what I have always wanted to do—start a hamburger joint?" Maybe you won't reach the top of your vocation, but at least you will be doing what you've always wanted to do.

## The "Squeeze Play" Syndrome

Another reason men are prone to reassess their jobs in the mid-life years is because they feel caught in what author Bob Briner calls "the squeeze play." Those of you who are *still* baseball fans understand what a squeeze play is. The runner on third is "squeezed home" by the batter trying to bunt. If all goes as planned, the runner scores. If the bunt doesn't work, the runner finds himself caught in a rundown between third and home.

Briner uses the analogy of "the squeeze play" to describe the tension that many men feel between work and family. Men in the mid-life years many times feel they are in a no-win situation with their job. Their work is the source of irritability, temptation, high blood pressure, and a less-than-suitable home life. Many men would love to give up their jobs or change vocations; yet they can't. They are trapped by their jobs. In the mid-life years they are probably at their peak earning years—which is good since they are also at their peak *spending* years. Saving for their children's education, braces, repairs on an increasingly older home, care for elderly parents, and underfunded retirement programs make it impossible for men to give up their jobs. Starting over in a new career would mean going to the bottom rung of the salary ladder—something most men cannot afford to do.

## The Reality Syndrome

A final reason that many men reevaluate their work during their mid-life years is the "reality syndrome." In their young adult years, men sometimes romanticize their professions. But after spending fifteen to twenty years in the same job, their eyes are opened. George Barna describes one man's collision with reality:

I came out of seminary anxious to save the world. Idealism isn't a bad thing; it can be a powerful motivation that helps you persevere in the face of calamity and trials. But, man, have I had my eyes opened in just twenty years.

I pastored a church, a small church, starting as an interim pastor, then becoming the permanent pastor when they asked me to stay and help heal the hurts that were there. I was there for five years. By then, I felt like I was swimming in molasses. People struggle with so much stuff, such deep stuff! I can't help them.

I was honest with them about it. I told them that I wasn't their solution, only God held the answers to their dilemmas, but that I'd do whatever I could to help them through it. But it was never enough, it was always a minute too late, it was . . . just overwhelming.

I finally had to leave the pastorate. It took me about four years to recover from what I'd been through in the ministry."[5]

Frankly, I hesitated using the above example because it was a "preacher illustration," and I realize that most of you reading this book are not paid clergymen. Yet I used it for just that reason. Most of my closest friends are not vocational ministers and so they really have an unrealistic view of a pastor's job. "I wish I had a job like yours where you knew you were making an eternal difference," one businessman recently lamented. He imagines that every hour of my day is spent leading people to Christ, miraculously mending broken homes, or listening to God's voice. If he only knew. Whether you are a minister, a doctor, a policeman, or an executive, there comes a time when you realize that your profession is not all you thought it would be. And that moment of reality usually arrives in the mid-life years.

I think that it is important to pause here for a moment and reiterate a truth we saw in chapter 2: There is nothing wrong with reevaluating any part of our lives—including our work. Our values may indeed change—and should change—as we realize our limited time on this planet is rapidly slipping away. Maybe we *should* switch jobs, or at least not devote as much energy toward our present one.

An honest assessment of your career may reveal that you will go no further in your chosen profession. If that is going to be a source of ongoing frustration, maybe this is the time to take a chance and start that greasy spoon restaurant.

As you consider the financial requirements of your family, you may come to the conclusion that you should stay in your current job. Or you may decide that some of those "requirements" are not worth mortgaging your health and happiness. By lowering your monthly "nut," you may discover that you could afford to change jobs.

The demythologization of your job may be the catalyst you need to make a career change. Or, it may open your eyes to the fact that your job was never intended to satisfy your deepest emotional and spiritual needs. That realization might encourage you to search for real fulfillment elsewhere.

## HOW TO EXPERIENCE CONTENTMENT IN YOUR CAREER

The mid-life years only become a "crisis" if we come to the wrong conclusions or make the wrong choices. Whatever decision the reevaluation of your career leads you to make, it is important that you learn the secret of contentment with your profession—whatever it is. How do you do that? Let me share with you five principles that will help you.

### Understand God's Attitude About Work

You will never enjoy your work as long as you see your job as:

   a. a necessary evil to help you pay the bills, or
   b. a way to mark time until retirement, or
   c. a hindrance to your spiritual service to God.

Yet many men have one or all of the above attitudes about their work. And some even try to use the Bible to support their belief that work is a curse. They point to Genesis 3:17–19 that records God's judgment against Adam and Eve, the earth, and the serpent: "'Cursed is the ground because of you; in toil you shall eat of it all the days of your life. Both thorns and thistles it shall grow for you; and you shall eat the plants of the field; by the sweat of your face you shall eat bread, till you return to the ground.'"

Seems clear, doesn't it? Work is God's way of getting even with us for our sin. "If only Adam had not allowed that woman to trick him into sinning (a true male perspective about the fall), I wouldn't have to roll out of bed tomorrow morning and go to that lousy job." That sounds logical until you consider one fact: God's command for man to work came *before* the fall. Before Eve took her first bite of that delicious piece of fruit, God had determined that man was to be a worker. For example, consider Genesis 1:26, 28: "Then God said, 'Let Us make man in Our image, according to Our likeness; and let them rule over the fish of the sea and over the birds of the sky and over the cattle and over all the earth. . . . And God blessed them; and God said to them, 'Be fruitful and multiply, and fill the earth, and subdue it; and rule over the fish of the sea and over the birds of the sky, and over every living thing that moves on the earth.'"

Or look at Genesis 2:8, 15: "And the LORD God planted a garden toward the east, in Eden; and there He placed the man whom He had formed. Then the LORD God took the man and put him into the garden of Eden to cultivate it and keep it."

Or again consider Solomon's words: "There is nothing better for a man than to eat and drink and tell himself that his labor is good. This also I have seen, that it is from the hand of God. For who can eat and who can have enjoyment without Him?" (Eccl. 2:24–25).

In their landmark book on a Christian view about work entitled *Your Work Matters to God,* Doug Sherman and William Hendricks point out two truths about work: (1) Man was created to be a worker. God's original plan for us was that we work. The garden of Eden was not an early version of Club Med. God's purpose for Adam was not that he enjoy an eternal life of leisure. The above passages show that Adam was created to work. In fact, as Solomon stated, work is a gift from God. Just as God is a worker (as evidenced by His creation), we are created in His image. That means we are created to work. We are never more like God than when we are working.

(2) Our work is an extension of God's work. Did you notice something about Genesis 2:8, 15? God created Eden without any help from anyone, but He created it in such a way that the garden was not self-sustaining. It still needed someone to "cultivate it and keep it." And that someone was Adam. Don't misunderstand. It is not that God *needed* Adam. Certainly He could have designed the earth so that it needed no human effort. Yet God chose to create the earth in a way that allows us to make our work a continuation of His work.

Your chosen vocation may have nothing to do with cultivating the ground, but it is still an extension of God's work. For example, part of God's work includes providing for the needs of His children. If your job in any way helps supply people with food, or clothing, or shelter, your work is an extension of His work.

Part of God's work involves executing justice against those who do evil. If you are involved in the legal system or in law enforcement, your work is an extension of God's work.

A man who supervised a crew for a moving company explained how his job was a part of his "religious mission": "Well, it's like this. Moving is hard for most people. It's a very vulnerable time for them. People are nervous about going to a new community, and about having strangers pack their most precious possessions. So, I think God wants me to treat my customers with love and to make them feel that I care about their things and their life. God wants me to help make their changes go smoothly."[6]

Get the picture? You don't have to be a pastor, evangelist, or missionary to be involved in God's work. God's work involves more than evangelism and discipleship. God calls men and women to a variety of positions to fulfill His purpose.[7]

### Choose the Right Career

Your job should allow you to exercise your God-given interests and abilities. If you choose a vocation that does not match your innate interests and abilities, you are doomed to a life of frustration. Perhaps you are familiar with the parable entitled "Animal School":

> The animals got together in the forest one day and decided to start a school. There was a rabbit, a bird, a squirrel, a fish, and an eel. They formed a board of education and tried to create a curriculum.
>
> The rabbit insisted that burrowing in the ground be in the curriculum. The fish insisted on swimming. The squirrel insisted that perpendicular tree climbing be included, and the bird wanted flying.
>
> They put all these courses together and wrote a curriculum guide. Then they insisted that all of the animals take all of the subjects.
>
> Although the rabbit was getting an A in burrowing, perpendicular tree climbing was a real problem for him; he kept falling over backwards. Pretty soon he became brain damaged from these falls, and he couldn't burrow well any more. He found that instead of making an A in burrowing, he was making a C. And, of course, he always made an F in perpendicular climbing.
>
> The bird was really beautiful at flying, but when it came to burrowing in the ground, he couldn't do it so well. He kept breaking his beak and wings. Pretty soon he was making a C in flying as well as an F in burrowing. And he had a very bad time with perpendicular tree climbing.
>
> The squirrel was terrific at perpendicular tree climbing, but was so afraid of the water that he failed swimming altogether.
>
> The fish was easily the best in swimming class, but he wouldn't get out of the water to come to any of the other classes.
>
> The valedictorian of the class was a mentally retarded eel who did everything in a halfway fashion. But the teachers were happy because everybody was taking all the subjects in their broad-based educational curriculum.[8]

Just as God has created animals with natural abilities, He has also given you unique interests and talents to fulfill His plan for your life. When you choose a vocation that does not maximize those gifts, you are working against God's plan for your life.

Maybe you feel like your job is not allowing you to maximize your gifts. Perhaps it *is* time for you to change careers. How can you make a wise decision about a move?

Recently my wife and I spent a week with Bobb Biehl. Bobb's specialty is knowing how to ask the right questions in any situation. In his superb booklet *100 Profound Questions,* Bobb suggests ten questions to ask anytime you are considering changing careers:

1. What do I see to be the major advantages of this career change? (Make an exhaustive list.)

2. Why am I thinking of this change? What is the real motive hidden deep in my heart where no one sees?

3. What is the real price or loss that comes with this change? (Make a list.) What may be eliminated if I talk with my team leaders? Is the tension at my present situation a temporary or a long-term problem?

4. Is the timing right for a move?

5. Where do I see myself in five to ten years? What is my overall career path? Does this change represent a step in the "right" direction for my long-range plans? What would I most like my epitaph to read? How would this change affect the totality of my lifework?

6. What do my three to five closest advisors think about the possible change? My spouse? My mentor?

7. How will the change affect the following areas:

   My spiritual development?
   My physical development?
   My personal development?
   My family/marriage relationship?

My social life?
My professional life?
My financial situation?

8. In what areas would I most like to grow personally and develop my full potential? Which opportunity offers me the most potential for growth in these areas?

9. What questions are lingering in my mind that should be asked before I make a final decision? What facts should I really see before I make the final decision?

10. What would I do if I had all the time, money, education, staff, etc. . . . and God said He didn't care what I did . . . and I knew I couldn't fail . . . what would I do?

Bobb suggests that you choose a career that allows you to expend 85 percent of your time maximizing your strengths and 15 percent working on your weaknesses. He then offers these words which should linger in our minds when evaluating a career: "Life is too short to work at something you don't enjoy, if you have a choice."[9]

### Maintain Balance in Your Work

If you are continually frustrated with your work, it may be because you are spending too much time at it. Charles Spurgeon once wrote, "All men must work, but no man should work beyond his physical and intellectual ability, nor beyond the hours which nature allots. No net result of good to the individual nor the race comes of any artificial prolonging of the day at either end. Work while it is day. When night comes, rest."[10] Let me suggest practical ways to maintain balance in your work:

*Refuse to work seven days a week.* The quickest way to burnout is to violate God's command about relaxation by laboring seven days a week. Isn't it interesting that God devotes more space to the fourth commandment than to any other? "Six days you shall labor and do all your work, but the seventh day is a sabbath of the LORD your God" (see Ex. 20:8–11). Although some men think it's kind of macho to see how much they can work, they need to realize that the sin of overwork ranks right up there with adultery, theft, idolatry, and murder. God commands that we take a mini-vacation each week from our work to remind us that there is more to life than our job.

*Refuse to take on a second job—unless absolutely necessary.* An increasing number of men are taking on extra jobs to generate additional income. They use their spare time to start a new business, work an additional shift, or become involved in a direct marketing scheme. Moonlighting is increasingly becoming a part of the American work scene. When workers at a rubber manufacturing plant in Ohio were given a six-hour workday, over half of them took on a second full- or part-time job."

In some cases the additional income may be truly needed. Many times, though, the additional money is used for discretionary purchases. The result is that some other area of our life gets short-changed—our family, our spiritual life, or our health. Solomon had some good words for anyone considering additional work: "Do not wear yourself out to get rich; have the wisdom to show restraint" (Prov. 23:4, NIV).

*Get involved in physical exercise.* Twenty minutes of vigorous exercise each day has a way of restoring perspective to my work and every other life area. Too busy to exercise you say? Consider the story of the woodsman who bought a brand new ax. The first day he was able to chop down twenty trees. With each passing day, he worked longer and harder, while chopping down fewer trees. A friend wandered by and suggested, "Why don't you sharpen your ax?" The woodsman replied, "I don't have time. I've got to chop down more trees!" Physical exercise is one of the best ways I know to "sharpen the ax." If you're too busy to exercise, then you're too busy!

*Make your family a part of your daily schedule.* Time with your wife and your children should be built into your daily calendar, just like any other important activity. One key to maintaining the proper perspective about your job is to never forget the reason you are working as hard as you are: to provide for that family you care so much about.

It is easy to allow our work to become an end in itself, rather than the means to an end. Just listen to those who made the mistake of allowing their work to take precedence over their family.

> "[My] greatest mistake was taking too many speaking engagements and not spending enough time with my family" (Evangelist Billy Graham).
>
> "My problem is, I operate in only two gears, overdrive and neutral, and it's all been overdrive since about 1982. . . . I had to return from it [a family ski trip] early and missed seeing my daughter in a race. I was in here at the office when the market was closed and the family was skiing and I said 'What am I doing? . . . I haven't been there for Beth, my seven-year old, either'" (Peter Lynch, author and investor).
>
> "Personally, I have learned the hard way that it is one grand illusion if you start believing you can be totally dedicated to the demands of your job without shortchanging your pressing responsibilities to your family" (Brandon Tartikoff, former chairman of Paramount Pictures).[12]

Following the above suggestions will help you maintain balance between your job and other important aspects of your life.

### Maintain the Proper Motivation in Your Work

I saw a book recently that captures the feeling of many employees: *How to Work for a Jerk*. Whether you are working for a jerk or working for yourself, it is sometimes difficult to remain enthusiastic about your job. But I have discovered a verse a Scripture that is a great motivation toward excellence in your job: "Whatever you do, do your work heartily, as for the Lord rather than for men; knowing that from the Lord you will receive the reward of the inheritance. It is the Lord Christ whom you serve" (Col. 3:23–24).

I want you to notice three truths in the above command.

*All work is important to God.* Whether your job is sitting in the executive suite, or sweeping it, your work has great value to God. *"Whatever* you do."

*Your ultimate boss is God.* You may think you are working for Mr. or Ms. X, or you may even think you are self-employed, but God is really your employer. "It is the Lord Christ whom you serve."

*Your ultimate compensation will come from God.* "Knowing that from the Lord you will receive the inheritance." Ray Steadman tells the story about an old missionary couple who were returning to New York to retire after years of labor in Africa. They had no pension, their health was broken, and they were discouraged. They discovered that President Teddy Roosevelt was booked on their ship, returning from one of his big-game hunting expeditions. Throughout the journey, no one paid any attention to the couple. They watched the fanfare that accompanied the President's entourage, with passengers eager to catch a glimpse of the returning hero. When the ship docked, a band and large crowd were there to carry the president away. No one was there to meet the missionary couple.

The old missionary said to his wife, "This is not right. Why should we have given our lives in faithful service to God and have no one care about us? Here this man comes back from a hunting trip and everybody makes much over him, but no one cares two hoots for us. At least someone should have been here to welcome us home." His wife gently replied, "But dear, we're not home, yet."

Unhappy about your pay? Feel unappreciated? Just wait. If you perform your work enthusiastically and for the right reason, God will generously compensate you for your efforts when you finally arrive home.

## Have a Life Purpose That Is Bigger Than Your Vocation

You've no doubt heard the story about the pedestrian who passed by three men who were laboring at the same job. "What are you doing?" The first workman answered, "I am laying stone." The second one replied, "I am erecting a wall." But the third one said, "I am building a cathedral." Even though they were performing the same task, they had a different perspective about their work.

Our work is an extension of God's work. Our jobs have value in and of themselves. One does not have to be constantly passing out tracts or preaching in the lunchroom to "redeem" his job. Your job is just as much a sacred calling from God as mine is.

Nevertheless, as Christians we must view our jobs through the lens of the Great Commission. Our primary objective should be to make disciples of Jesus Christ. That means introducing unbelievers to the gospel and helping believers mature in their faith. Our jobs many times provide a platform from which to perform our ministry.

One man who understands this truth is Norman Miller, president of Interstate Batteries. Every Monday morning his employees show up at work an hour early for the weekly, voluntary Bible study. They pray that God will help them to become more committed to their family, to their country, and to their job of selling car batteries. Miller explains how his faith and vocation relate to one another. "I need to be faithful to Jesus 100 percent of the time, and that includes my business." To do his part in fulfilling the Great Commission, Miller has spent $3 million of his fortune to distribute the "Jesus" video around the world. He also donates a large amount of money to help elect political candidates who will further Christian principles in our nation. Norm Miller is just one of an increasing number of people who are discovering how their work is but one component of a bigger life purpose.[13]

The restlessness you feel from your job may be an indicator that it is time to move to another career. Maybe there is a job out there that would better utilize your gifts and interests. Or, it could be that your dissatisfaction with your work is a signal that you are spending too much time on the job and need to gain more balance in your life.

But possibly your discontent is fueled by an unrealistic expectation: depending on your job to fill your need for significance. Bob Buford, author of the excellent book *Half Time,* says, "One of the most common characteristics of a person nearing the end of the first half [of the game of life] is that unquenchable desire to move from success to significance."[14] When we, like Norman Miller, dedicate our lives to a purpose that is bigger than our work, we will experience significance and, therefore, a higher level of satisfaction from our work.

## FOR FURTHER REFLECTION

1. In what ways have your values changed in the past twenty years? How have these changes affected your attitude about your job?

2. Do you see yourself staying in the same job for the rest of your working years? Why or why not?

3. If you could have any job in the world, what would it be? What barriers are preventing you from that job?

4. How could your job be viewed as an extension of God's work?

5. Would your wife, children, and friends say that you work too little or too much? If the consensus is too much, what practical steps can you take to correct the situation?

# CHAPTER SIX

## Seeing God's Hand
## in Your Spouse

**M**y first date with Amy occurred when we were both in the ninth grade. Since we were too young to drive, my parents chauffeured us to the El Fenix Mexican restaurant in Dallas and then to the Esquire theater to see the movie *My Fair Lady*. This wonderful musical about an English professor who tries to remake a common street girl is based on the play *Pygmalion*. Pygmalion was a Cyprian king who suffered a malady common to many men—he could not find the perfect woman. So he decided to sculpt his own out of ivory. He spent months chiseling away every imperfection. Once he had finished his creation, he bowed his head and begin to pray. Miraculously, the statue came to life and Pygmalion and his "statuesque" wife lived happily ever after.

Sitting in that darkened theater more than twenty-five years ago, watching Rex Harrison and Audrey Hepburn's musical version of this well-worn literary theme, I was sure I had found my perfect match. No chiseling necessary. After the credits rolled and the lights came up, Amy and I dutifully arose from our seats and were carried with the stream of people to the back of the auditorium. Knowing that my parents were waiting outside and there would be no opportunity for any private communication in the car, I summoned every bit of courage I had and took the biggest chance of my life.

"Amy, could you wait up just a minute? I have something I want to talk to you about. I have a problem and don't know what to do about it."

"What is it, Robert?"

"There's this, uh, girl I like very much, but I don't know, uh, how to tell her."

"Is it someone I know?" (We went to the same school and had almost every class together.)

"Yes, her name is Amy."

"Amy Anderson?" (one of three "Amys" in our class).

"No, it is you—Amy Renard."

Cue the violins. I don't remember much about the ride home in our Buick station wagon, other than staring at one another in silence. My mom would tell me years later that she knew something significant had happened in that theater. I walked Amy to her front steps, we pledged to talk to one another the next day, and I returned home, ready to break into my own rendition of "I Could Have Danced All Night." Thus began my pursuit of and eventual marriage to Amy Lyon Renard.

I was attracted to Amy because she was different from any other girl I had met. She was beautiful; she possessed a keen wit; she was intelligent; she could care less what other people thought about her. And most importantly, she thought I was wonderful. What more could a guy want?

And yet, over the years of our courtship and marriage, there have been times when I have taken for granted and even have tried to change those qualities that originally attracted me to her. I don't think I am alone in this. Few men ever escape a time of serious reevaluation of their marriage and their marriage partner:

- "If only she were more like _____."
- "If only she were less _____."
- "Is this the person I really want to be with the rest of my life?"
- "I wonder what life would have been like had I married _____."

As we have seen in previous chapters, the reevaluation of any life area can be enormously productive, leading to an even deeper commitment to our core values and choices. Unfortunately, some reevaluations lead to erroneous conclusions and disastrous consequences.

Yesterday, a man came to see me. He has been married twenty years and has suddenly realized that he is no longer happy in the relationship. "In fact," he admitted, "I haven't been happy in ten years. So I told my wife last night that I have been living a lie and want out of the relationship." I spent almost two hours reminding him that as a professing Christian he had to consider other issues besides being "happy." I reminded him of the unconditional vow he had made to God. I pointed out the indelible mark a divorce would leave on his young daughter. As a last resort, I warned him of the severe financial hardship of trying to support two households. But neither his faith, nor his family, nor his finances were enough to keep him from dissolving his marriage in the search for something better.

What is it that causes a man to renounce his spiritual convictions, reject his wife, abandon his children, and risk financial impoverishment for an untested relationship with another woman that may or may not work out? In this chapter we are going to examine the sources of discontent in marriage and then look at some practical ways to see God's plan in your marriage.

## SECOND THOUGHTS

### Changes in Emotional Needs

When Ted and Janet met in college over twenty years ago, Janet was a senior undergraduate student and Ted was in law school. Throughout their courtship, Ted did a terrific job of balancing his study schedule, part-time work, and his pursuit of his future wife. Once they graduated, they married and he began his work as a junior partner in a growing firm. It was not uncommon for Ted to work sixty and seventy hours a week while Janet tried to fill her days by reading or decorating their small apartment. Unexpectedly, she became pregnant and soon she did not have to worry about filling her time. Nevertheless, she eagerly anticipated Ted's arrival home each evening. She needed someone to talk with.

Unfortunately, Ted usually had a number of calls to return when he arrived home, or was just too exhausted for any meaningful conversation. He needed some "down time" to read the paper, pursue his golf hobby, or just sit and stare at the television set. This pattern continued throughout their first fifteen years of marriage: Ted pouring all of his energy into his career and Janet feeling resentful of playing second fiddle to her husband's vocation.

Ted just recently celebrated his fortieth birthday. Although his friends have mercilessly kidded him about being "over the hill" and having "one foot in the grave," Ted is finding little to laugh about as he enters the "noon" of his life. He has suddenly discovered (or rediscovered) his need for intimacy with other people. A serious inventory of his relationships revealed that he has no one who he feels really loves him or understands him. His wife long ago quit trying to enter his private world—not because she didn't love him, but the continual rejection was just too painful for her to handle.

Now that the kids are in high school, Janet has a lot of time on her hands. She began a part-time career several years ago as an interior decorator. She is active in her church and civic groups. She has filled the emotional vacuum in her life with activity.

And so, there has been a reversal of emotional needs in this relationship. Ted spent the first two decades of his marriage suppressing his emotional relationships in order to build a career. But as he enters mid-life, he is doing some serious reevaluation of his life. After years of performing the same task, a man may hit the glass ceiling, realizing there are no more chances for promotion. Or he may simply view his work more realistically, removing the rose-colored glasses that he wore during the early years of his job. Regardless of the motivation, the bottom-line conclusion is the same. "I don't want to mortgage the rest of my life for this job. I need someone I can talk to. Someone who loves me and accepts me for who I am."

So where does Ted go to meet that emotional need he has successfully suppressed for twenty years? His children have lives of their own. His wife has found emotional fulfillment in her own career and activities. But there is the twenty-three-year-old female clerk in his firm's legal library that thinks Ted is pretty wonderful. She laughs at all of his jokes. She marvels that he has achieved so much in his short career. She compliments him on his wardrobe. She suggests that maybe they could have lunch together.

The trite conclusion to this story would be that they hop in the sack, fall madly in love, and Ted leaves Janet to marry this woman almost half his age. That may or may not happen. But what is *sure* to happen is that Ted will grow increasingly discontented with his wife. He will begin to compare this young girl's attentiveness to his wife's disinterest. Ted's once dormant emotional needs have been awakened and he feels desperate to have them fulfilled.

### Sexual Boredom

Another reason that men reevaluate their marriages is boredom in the bedroom. Take a moment to do an honest evaluation of your sex life. Do you and your wife make love as often as you did when you were first married? Do you and your wife look forward to sex or view it as a "duty"? Do you occasionally have problems with impotence? Masters and Johnsons have identified six conditions that contribute to a man's diminishing interest in sex during the mid-life years:

1. Monotony of a repetitious relationship.
2. Preoccupation with career or economic pursuits.
3. Mental or physical fatigue.
4. Overindulgence in food or drink.

5. Physical and mental infirmities of a man or his spouse.
6. Fear of failure in the sex act.[1]

While there are definitely some physiological changes that may retard a man's sexual appetite, notice that many of the above factors deal with emotional issues: monotony, preoccupation, fatigue, and fear. If these issues are resolved, there is no reason a man cannot enjoy a satisfying sex life throughout most of his life.

But there is also a dangerous corollary here. Men (and women) are sexual creatures. We have needs that we *will* eventually meet. If these emotional barriers to a satisfying sexual relationship are not removed within the context of a marriage, they may be resolved in a relationship *outside* the marriage. On many occasions I have heard men involved in affairs exclaim, "She makes me feel young again"; "I forget about everything whenever I am with her"; "She does things my wife would never do."

What has caused these once latent desires to suddenly come alive? Nothing has changed physiologically. But *much* has changed emotionally. A man involved in an illicit relationship is forced to expend a great deal of energy, time, and creativity in initiating and maintaining a new romance. In fact, it is the same kind of energy, time, and creativity he once spent on his wife during their years of dating and early marriage. The result? The husband is enjoying the same sexual excitement with his new "squeeze" that he once experienced with his mate.

### Availability of Options

One successful builder explained this phenomenon to me this way. When he was just starting out in his business, he and his wife were struggling financially, he was trying to build a reputation, and he had three small children at home. In his mind, he really did not have that many choices to make in life. He went to work, came home, and hoped that his business would one day thrive.

Now he has arrived. His business is booming, his portfolio is bulging, and his last child is leaving for college next year. For years he has felt trapped in a loveless marriage. He felt like his marriage was his "cross to bear" and was willing to endure it rather than to go through a painful divorce—a divorce that might leave him lonely and bankrupt.

But now he realizes he has other choices. There is a secretary in his office who has aroused his interest. He often fantasizes about leaving his wife, selling his business, and sailing around the world with his secretary on his forty-two-foot sailboat. Guess what? What once was an impossible dream is a very real possibility. He's already made his professional mark—nothing left to prove there. His children are just about gone—he's done about all he can do with them. He could close his business right now, split his assets down the middle with his wife, and still have enough income to live. And the secretary is more than willing.

One benefit of growing older is that many times we do have more options—vocational options, economic options, geographic options. In light of these increasing choices, it can be a healthy exercise to ask yourself:

- "Why not try my hand at a new job for a few years? I'm not attached to my profession."
- "Why not retire early, or at least cut down my hours? I've been able to save some money, so I don't have to worry about starving to death."
- "Why not move to _____? My kids are grown, my house is paid for, and my wife is agreeable."

But in all of these reevaluations it is important to correctly label what things are optional and what are nonoptional. At the top of the list of those decisions which are nonoptional is remaining with our mate.

Solomon had many different options in life. His power and wealth afforded him with numerous choices. During one period in his life, he took full advantage of those opportunities, accumulating seven hundred wives and three hundred concubines. Yet the wisest man who ever lived confessed that none of those liaisons fulfilled him. His advice? "Rejoice in the wife of your youth. As a loving hind and a graceful doe, let her breasts satisfy you at all times; be exhilarated always with her love. For why should you, my son, be exhilarated with an adulteress, and embrace the bosom of a foreigner?" (Prov. 5:18–20).

## REJOICE IN THE WIFE OF YOUR YOUTH

For many men that is easier said than done. How can a man experience joy, satisfaction, and even exhilaration in a marriage that is decades old?

### Eliminate Your Options

You probably remember the story of the Spanish explorer Hernando Cortés. He was attracted to the promise of vast wealth in Mexico and persuaded the Spanish governor to give him eleven ships and seven hundred men for the journey. Maybe after spending several months locked up with these men sailing the high seas, Cortés begin to sense that his men were not quite as committed to the project as he was. Cortés knew enough about the hardships they would encounter in this treacherous land to understand this was no time for half-hearted commitment. So he instigated what may be the first "incentive program" in the history of North American labor relations. As soon as all of the ships were unloaded, Cortés ordered all of the ships burned.

No matter how difficult their expedition became, no matter how insurmountable the odds, Cortés and his men were forced to be totally committed to the venture's success. There were no other options. No escape route.[2]

We must be equally committed to the success of our marriages. And the best way to ensure success is to eliminate our other options. We must remove the words *affair, divorce,* and *remarriage* from our emotional vocabulary. We must resolve that our emotional and physical needs are going to be met by our wives—or they will not be met at all. That kind of commitment is a great incentive to make our marriages work.

Many times I have dealt with situations where a husband suddenly moved out of his home, requesting a "trial separation" from his wife. When pinned down about why he left, he vaguely responds that his needs have not been met and he just needs some time to "sort things out." Although his wife is devastated, she takes comfort in his pledge that there is not another woman involved. But within a few months the deserted wife is horrified to discover that there *is* another woman.

I'm *never* surprised. I know men well enough to know that we are too selfish to go any amount of time without some sexual and emotional fulfillment. If you told a man contemplating leaving his wife and family that if he left he would have a scarlet "A" stamped on his forehead, and he would thus be prohibited from having sex or any meaningful communication with a woman for the rest of his life, I guarantee you he would rethink his decision. He would suddenly discover that things at home were not as bad as he supposed. Why? His options have been eliminated.

As disciples of Jesus Christ, when we married, we burned the ships. God's Word eliminates all options for divorce and subsequent remarriage (with the possible exception of our mate's adultery or desertion). Consider what God's Word says about divorce:

> "Because the LORD has been a witness between you and the wife of your youth, against whom you have dealt treacherously, though she is your companion and your wife by covenant. . . . For I hate divorce," says the LORD, the God of Israel, "and him who covers his garment with wrong," says the LORD of hosts. (Mal. 2:14, 16)
>
> "For this cause a man shall leave his father and mother, and shall cleave to his wife; and the two shall become one flesh. Consequently they are no longer two, but one flesh. What therefore God has joined together, let no man separate." (Matt. 19:5–6)
>
> "And I say to you, whoever divorces his wife, except for immorality, and marries another woman commits adultery." (Matt. 19:9)

My purpose in citing these verses is not to lay a guilt trip on you, especially if you have already divorced and/or remarried. But these verses should remind you that whether you are in your first or seventh marriage, divorce is no longer an option for you as long as you are a serious disciple of Christ. Only when you reach that conclusion and remove the "change your partner do-si-do" option, will you ever be able to experience contentment with your wife.

## Appreciate Your Wife's Uniqueness

The story of Pygmalion, the king who created his perfect mate, is a myth; yet the story is not as far-fetched as you might think. Genesis 2 indicates that every woman is perfectly "built"—not by us, but by God: "Then the LORD God said, 'It is not good for the man to be alone; I will make him a helper suitable for him.' And the LORD God fashioned into a woman the rib which He had taken from the man, and brought her to the man" (2:18, 22).

Several important principles emerge from this passage:

*Man is incomplete without a woman.* Isn't it interesting that God said that it was unacceptable for Adam to be "alone"? Adam was anything but alone. There was a garden filled with plants and animals to keep him occupied. More importantly, Adam was enjoying a perfect relationship with his Creator, since the serpent had not entered the picture. Yet God said that neither a man's work nor even his spiritual life was enough. He needed another human with whom to share his life.

*Women are designed to complement, not duplicate, men.* It has been my observation that at the core of most marital conflicts is one spouse trying to make the other spouse like himself/herself. If a husband is an extrovert and his wife is an introvert, he hammers away at his wife to be more "friendly" or "outgoing." If a husband is spontaneous and his wife is methodical, he chides his wife to "loosen up." If a man is frugal with his money and has married a spender, he can't understand why his wife can't be more "reasonable" with the checkbook.

However, God never intended for our spouse to be a carbon copy of ourselves. The *New International Version* translates Genesis 2:18 this way: "I will make a helper suitable for him." The Hebrew word translated "suitable" literally means "opposite." God wanted to bring someone into your life who could shore up the weaknesses in your life. You see, in order to be properly balanced in life—to really enjoy life to the fullest—extroverts need some time to be introspective. Savers need to loosen the purse strings occasionally. And our spontaneity needs to be coupled with some serious planning. God's plan is to bring us a mate who is able to complement, not duplicate, our deficiencies.

*God has uniquely created your wife.* Genesis 2:22 states that the Lord God "fashioned into a woman the rib which He had taken from the man." The word translated *fashioned* comes from the Hebrew word that literally means "built." God built Eve! He started with nothing but a rib and designed such a beautiful creation that when Adam first saw her he exclaimed "WOW!" (that's Hebrew for "This is now bone of my bones, and flesh of my flesh").

I do not believe that God's creative work ended with Eve. Psalm 139 is used by many to denounce abortion or to bolster a sagging self-image. But instead of thinking of a fetus or even yourself, insert the name of your wife into this passage:

> For Thou didst form _____'s inward parts;
> Thou didst weave _____ in [her]
>     mother's womb.
> I will give thanks to Thee, for _____ [is]
>     fearfully and wonderfully made;
>     Wonderful are Thy works,
>     And my soul knows it very well.
>
>                   (Ps. 139:13–14)

In order to bring these truths from the theoretical to the practical, let me encourage you to do something. Take just a moment right now to make a list of the five things you most appreciate about your wife. Then, take your wife out to dinner this week (please leave your book at home so that this looks somewhat spontaneous) and tell her the five things you most appreciate about her.

WHAT I MOST APPRECIATE ABOUT _____

1.

2.

3.

4.

5.

## Make Your Marriage a Priority

I asked one of our older deacons who has discipled and mentored dozens of younger men why he thought so many men were discontented with their marriages. "Pastor, many men treat their wives like a piece of chicken. They pick, pick, pick, 'til there's nothing left except the bone, and then they throw away the bone." I'd never thought of it that way before, but it is true. We often fail to understand that a marriage is what J. Allan Petersen calls an "empty box." Read the following quotation very carefully. This concept alone is worth the price of this book!

> Dr. Willard Beecher tells how most people come to marriage believing it is a box full of goodies from which we extract all we need to make us happy. The marriage license is also the key to this box. We can take from it as much as we want and it somehow mysteriously remains full. And even when the box does get empty and the marriage collapses in a heap, we have not learned our lesson. We still look for a second partner that will bring another bottomless box with him so we can empty it.
>
> Marriage is an empty box. There's nothing in it. It is an opportunity to put something in, to do something for marriage. Marriage was never intended to do anything

for anybody. People are expected to do something for marriage. If you do not put into the box more than you take out, it becomes empty. Love isn't in marriage, it is in people, and people put it into marriage. Romance, consideration, generosity aren't in marriage, they are in people, and people put them into the marriage box. When the box gets empty we become vulnerable for an affair.[3]

Consider the amount of time and emotional energy you are pouring into your job. Now you probably can already tell where I'm going with this. What if you expended that same time and energy on strengthening your marriage? "That's not fair, Robert. I don't have a choice about my job. I *have* to work as hard as I do in today's cut-throat environment. If I don't, I won't have a job." That may very well be true. But if you don't also expend some effort filling the "empty box" of your marriage relationship, you won't have a marriage, either. If you don't believe me, ask Pat Williams, general manager for the Orlando Magic.

In the early 1980s Pat was the general manager of the champion Philadelphia 76ers basketball team. All of his energy was directed toward building a successful franchise. But on December 19, 1982, Pat's wife, Jill, informed him that she didn't love him any longer and wanted out of the marriage. Suddenly, Pat's career was not nearly as important as it once was. In their excellent book *Rekindled,* Pat and Jill relate how Pat rebuilt the relationship he had so easily taken for granted.

In the book he shares four principles he learned from marriage counselor Dr. Ed Wheat about how to transform a stale or decaying marriage. Dr. Wheat calls them the BEST principles. These are principles any man can use to fill the "empty box."

## **B**less Your Spouse

Dr. Wheat encouraged Pat to "bless" his wife in four specific ways: (1) to speak well of her, (2) to do kind things for her, (3) to express thanksgiving for her verbally, and (4) to pray for her good.

As Pat shares his story with other men, he now encourages every man who wants to improve his relationship to take "the ninety-day test." "You must go ninety straight days during which you respond with kind, uplifting, encouraging words to everything that comes your way, good or bad. If you blow it, you start over at day one and shoot for ninety again."[4]

## *Edify* Your Spouse

To "edify" means to build up. One strong way we strengthen our wives is through sincere and frequent verbal praise. When we give verbal praise to our wife and speak well of her to others, we are recognizing her value. The primary reason for praising our wives is to encourage them. But a secondary benefit of verbal praise is that it reinforces to us the uniqueness and value of our spouse. Proverbs 31 describes the "excellent wife." She is industrious, beautiful, trustworthy, and supportive of her husband. Some men might read the passage and think, "If only my wife were like that." But I want you to notice what has contributed to this wife's excellence: "Her husband also [blesses her], and he praises her, saying 'Many daughters have done nobly, but you excel them all'" (31:28–29). The husband of the "excellent wife" is diligent to praise his mate, and the results are obvious.

## *Share* with Your Spouse

Dr. Wheat challenges men to share time, hobbies, interests, their innermost thoughts, and their goals with their wives—and allow their wives to do the same with them. If we are not careful, it is easy for our home to become nothing more than a bed and breakfast joint where we stop in for food, a night's rest, and a change of clothes before resuming our "real lives." Let me suggest several practical ways to build intimacy with your wife. Not all of them will be applicable to your situation, but some of them will.

*Take a day off each week to devote to your wife and children.* God never intended for us to work seven days a week. When you violate this command, you are not only cheating yourself, but you are robbing your family of time they need to spend with you.

*Take your wife on business trips with you.* This is something I am doing more frequently. Yes, it is expensive and sometimes inconvenient (especially having to arrange child-care for small children), but it is worth the money and effort. I have discovered that taking my wife with me on trips gives her a break from her routine, allows us to spend some quality time talking with one another, and permits her to enter my world for a few days—something she wants to do.

*Take advantage of opportunities to "retune" your marriage.* As I write these words, our church is preparing to host a "Home Improvements Marriage Seminar" with Dr. Howard Hendricks, one of America's foremost authorities on the family. Those of you who have heard Dr. Hendricks or read his books know firsthand what a dynamic communicator he is. Yet our staff is having to figure out how to motivate people—especially men— to attend the conference. Golf games, out-of-town trips, soccer tournaments, or mundane errands are viewed as "essential," while a weekend spent improving the most foundational relationship of our lives is seen as "optional." Let me encourage you to commit to participating with your wife in one activity a year to strengthen your relationship. Your church, denomination, or some other Christian organization is sure to offer a seminar or retreat you can participate in. It will be well worth the money and time.

## Touch Your Spouse

When Dr. Wheat writes about touching, he is referring to non-sexual physical contact: holding hands, hugging, and caressing. This kind of contact is important for calming fears, soothing pain, and building emotional security.[5] But I would expand this principle to include the sexual aspect of marriage as well.

I was talking with a friend of mine last week about my ideas for this chapter. My friend is highly successful and well educated.

However, when we started talking about the problem of sexual boredom in marriage, he commented, "That is a real cause of discontent. I know this is going to sound sexist, but I think it is mainly the wife's fault. If they were more creative, then we wouldn't be so tempted to wander off."

So much for the "age of enlightenment." If we are going to keep the physical part of our relationship exhilarating, we must be willing to take the initiative in improving our sexual relationship with our wives. Space does not permit us to address that subject here, but there are a plethora of Christian books available on the subject, including Ed Wheat's *Intended for Pleasure,* which I frequently use in counseling.

### Fail to Fall for the "Grass Is Greener" Myth

The realization that there are no other options can be a powerful incentive for choosing to be content in our relationship. But how do you really "burn the ships"—especially when so many seem to be floating by every day at work, at church, or in our neighborhood. Many men who understand all the biblical admonitions against divorce and remarriage still bail out of marriages everyday, hoping to find the physical and emotional fulfillment they crave.

What causes them to suddenly discard their entire value system for an untested relationship? How are they so easily duped? They are the victims of one of Satan's oldest and most effective schemes. James exposes the lie this way: "But each one is tempted when he is carried away and enticed by his own lust" (James 1:14). The word translated *enticed* is a fishing term that means "hooked." The picture here is of a fisherman who knows exactly what bait to dangle in front of a hungry and an unsuspecting fish. The fish, blinded by its own needs, bites into the lure, not knowing there is a hook in the middle that will carry it to its death.

In the same way, Satan is a master fisherman. He knows what "bait" to dangle in front of us. It may be a woman who arouses us physically. Sometimes it is a woman who appeals to us emotionally—she has a similar sense of humor or provides the kind of emotional support we need. Unfortunately, some men who are starving to death emotionally and physically get "hooked" and the result is destruction. No matter how appealing that bait is, it has a hook in the middle of it! Solomon, who by his own admission allowed illicit relationships to destroy his life, observed: "For on account of a harlot one is reduced to a loaf of bread, and an adulteress hunts for the precious life. Can a man take fire in his bosom, and his clothes not be burned? Or can a man walk on hot coals, and his feet not be scorched? So is the one who goes in to his neighbor's wife; whoever touches her will not go unpunished" (Prov. 6:26–29).

Although Satan loves to entice us (and ultimately destroy us) by the promise of something better, God has already provided us with the perfect companion. When I find myself tempted by the "grass is greener" myth, I remember the saying, "If the grass is greener in someone else's pasture, it may be because his pasture is better cared for."

I love the story of Ali Hafed. He was a Persian who owned a very large farm, filled with orchards, grain fields, and gardens. One day Ali was visited by a Buddhist priest who told him that in spite of his wealth, he still lacked the greatest treasure of all—diamonds. He explained to Ali that these rare gems were the passport to everything he wanted for himself and his family.

From that point on, all Ali Hafed could dream about was diamonds. In his own mind, he became poor because he lacked that which the priest told him was the most valuable commodity of all. He sold his farm and took his family with him all over Palestine and Europe in search of diamonds. As he stood on the seashore in Barcelona, Spain, destitute and broken, he cast himself into the sea, never to be seen again.

The man who had purchased Ali Hafed's farm took his camel to a garden brook for a drink of water. The man noticed a brilliant flash of light from the brook. Reaching into the stream, he scooped up dozens of brilliant diamonds. The farmer had uncovered the Golconda mine—the largest diamond mine in history. Ali Hafed was richer than he ever thought. The diamonds he so desperately wanted were in his own backyard.

The secret to finding contentment in your marriage is to realize that you already have a diamond mine in your home. You don't need to search anywhere else for fulfillment. Your wife is a "crown jewel" to be valued above all others.[6]

## FOR FURTHER REFLECTION

1. Recall your dating experience with your wife. Name three qualities that first attracted you to your wife.

2. Which aspects of your life are changeable? Which are unchangeable? Why?

3. What are some practical things you could do this week to fill the "empty box" of your marriage?

4. Identify any potential "bait" that Satan may be dangling in front of you right now. What are some practical ways you can prevent getting "hooked"?

5. Can you see how God supernaturally brought you and your wife together? Explain.

# CHAPTER SEVEN

## Seeing God's Hand in Your Children

**M**any years ago a well-known troupe of tightrope walkers made the front page of the newspaper. The Flying Wallendas were performing their famous "incredible human pyramid" at Cobo Hall in Detroit when tragedy struck. The human pyramid consisted of four men walking across the high wire, supporting three more men standing on poles that were mounted to the walker's shoulder. Above those three men was a woman seated in a chair. What an act!

That night, as the "pyramid" inched its way across the wire, Dieter Wallenda's knees began to quiver. He yelled out, "I can't hold on any longer," and suddenly the entire pyramid collapsed. Most of the family members were thrown to the floor and suffered permanent injuries. A few hung on to the high wire until they were rescued. But no one present in the audience that night soon forgot the horrifying image of seeing a family suddenly destroyed.[1]

Maybe you are at the stage in your life when you can sympathize with Dieter Wallenda. You feel as if the entire weight of your family is resting upon your shoulders. As you move toward the middle of your life, the pressure seems to be increasing. Job demands are accelerating while the options for change are diminishing. Your family's expanding financial needs are outpacing your stagnant salary. Your aging parents are becoming increasingly dependent on you for physical, financial, and emotional support. And internally, you are trying to come to grips with the fact that many of your life dreams will never be realized.

Now, if that isn't enough to make your knees buckle, let me add one other weight to your shoulders: your children. "Oh, no," you protest. "My children are not a problem, they are a pleasure. They make life worth living." I have no doubt that is true—at times. As I write these words, I am looking at a picture of my two beautiful daughters, and I am bemoaning the fact that I must stay late at church tonight instead of going home to play with them.

But if I am honest, I will also have to admit that my children are also a source of very real pressure—pressure that forces me to reevaluate my life at times. Maybe you can identify with author Paul Lewis who describes what it is like to come home from work preoccupied or exhausted. "Simply reminding yourself that the reason you go to work is to support your family doesn't automatically give you the energy to actually enjoy your time with them. You may even look for a retreat from your children—which is ironic considering that they are the supposed pay-off for all your hard work. Sooner or later, every father wonders if this is all he is: Someone who works to provide for a family he doesn't have the time or energy to enjoy."[2]

The thesis of this book is that every man goes through a period of reevaluating each area of his life: his marriage, his work, his finances, his friendships, *and* his relationship with his children. Such reevaluations do not have to produce a crisis, but can actually be beneficial if they lead to the right conclusions or corrections.

Why would a man need to reassess his role as a father? Consider the following issues fathers confront:

- balancing the time demands of work and parenting
- providing financially for the needs/wants of our children
- trying to motivate our children to love and obey God
- accepting the physical and/or mental limitations of our children
- responding in a loving but firm way to a rebellious child
- coping with our children's departure from home

These are the very real issues most fathers face—this is "the road most traveled." However, I don't believe these issues have to crush our shoulders or buckle our knees if we are able to view our parenting responsibilities from God's perspective. The key to discovering the power of contentment is to be able to see God's hand in every area of our lives—including our children.

## I'D LIKE TO BE A FATHER BUT . . .

But before we look at some ways to experience contentment with our children, let's explore more carefully some of the issues confronting fathers during the mid-life years.

### Inadequate Time

One family expert says that he often asks men to name their greatest frustrations as a father. He claims that the most common answers are a variation on the theme of their lack of time:

- Not enough time with their children,
- Trying to get away from their jobs so they can have time with their kids,
- Finding constructive ways to use the small amount of time they have with their kids.

One dad expressed his frustration this way, "I feel like I'm swimming against a river of things that are demanding my time, struggling to get to the island where my children are waiting."[3]

Some of the time pressures men face are the result of the natural rhythm of life. During the first half of a man's career, fourteen-hour work days, missed weekends, and sporadic vacations are expected. It's the price we must pay to build a successful career and, thus, adequately provide for our family. It is unfortunate that the years during which a father is building his career often coincide with the years his children need him most.

Ironically, when a father finally wakes up to the fact that his career is not worth sacrificing his family for and desires to start spending more time with his kids, it is often too late. Like wives, children learn to cope with a father's physical and/or emotional absence and don't always respond positively to a father's sudden change of heart. Friends, hobbies, extracurricular activities have long since filled the void of an absent dad. Why should these kids suddenly give up those interests to spend time with a virtual stranger? This phenomena results in an emotional crisis for many fathers: "Why should I beat my brains out to provide for kids who will barely speak to me anymore?"

### Insufficient Money

Last night my wife came into the den with an announcement: our two girls needed new dresses and new shoes for Easter. Although I love to see my girls dressed up, this presented a dilemma for me. We had the money, but I had earmarked the funds for something else—a new suit for me. No, this was not a luxury (at least in my mind). I was getting ready to leave on a promotional tour for one of my books and needed to look my best. That would help sell more books and provide more income for my family. Right? For some reason that line of reasoning didn't wash with Amy. She reassured me that I looked just fine in my navy blue suit I purchased several years ago. And what kind of father would allow his children to walk around in ill-fitting clothes?

Last night's minor domestic crisis illustrates another "balancing act" fathers must perform in the mid-life years: the proper allocation of financial resources. Children represent a severe (and increasing) drain on the incomes of fathers who are approaching the zenith of their earning potential. Clothes, braces, cars, college expenses are just some of the endless needs of our children. How can we ever hope to pay for all of these costs and still fulfill some of the dreams we have like . . .

- early retirement from the job we hate, or
- an around-the-world cruise with our mate, or
- a second home at the lake.

Don't we deserve *some* pleasures in life? Must we *always* be the human sacrifice for our kids?

## Unmet Expectations

We all have certain expectations of our children. We dream of Johnny being the high school quarterback or Mary becoming a concert pianist. Sometimes our dreams for our children originate from a sincere desire to see them maximize opportunities that we never had. Other times, however, our expectations come from the attempt to relive our childhood and adolescence through our children. Regardless of the source, if we are not careful those expectations can rob us of contentment and place unbearable stress on our kids.

I've been reading an excellent book by Dr. Ralph Minear and William Proctor entitled *Kids Who Have Too Much*. The authors cite convincing data to demonstrate the relationship between parental expectations and childhood stress that manifests itself in everything from minor illnesses to substance abuse. They note that many parents are intent on "hothousing" their children. Just as some people use a greenhouse which is artificially kept at a high temperature to accelerate and maximize the growth of plants, some parents create a high-stress environment to maximize their children's performance, rather than allow them to develop at a relaxed pace. The authors mention three signs of "hothousing"— that is, placing too much stress on your children:

*Sign #1: Most of your child's day is booked up.* After spending a full day at school, Billy or Susie are whisked off to tennis practice or a soccer game. By the time practice is over, no one feels like preparing (or waiting for) a full supper, so the family dashes though McDonald's for a quick burger. When they get home, it's time for homework or an hour's worth of piano practice. The kids finally fall into bed exhausted, knowing that they have another full day ahead of them. Many experts say that children, especially young ones, need at least an hour or two each day of unscheduled time to relax and to exercise their creativity through free play.

*Sign #2: You enroll your toddler or preschooler in one or more early formal instruction programs.* An increasing number of experts are questioning the value of trying to teach toddlers how to read, or signing two- and three-year-olds up for music or swimming lessons. Every child should be treated as an individual. If they show a propensity—and more importantly, a desire—to engage in these instructional programs, fine. But parents need to honestly evaluate their motives in pushing their children to participate in these activities. Are their children really interested in them, or is the parent trying to live out his own desires through the child?

*Sign #3: The parent enrolls the child, at whatever age, in programs designed to provide a special advantage over other youngsters.* It is natural for parents to want to prove that their children are above average. One way to validate that their kids have indeed come from a superior gene pool is to push them into accelerated educational programs. William Kristol, a former Harvard professor and chief of staff to former U. S. Education Secretary William Bennett, observes, "Parents think if their children are not multiplying by age four, they won't get into Harvard by age eighteen. Our sense is that the evidence does not support that. There's too much pressure on parents."[4]

And that pressure is transferred to kids. If for some reason the child does not do well in these advanced programs, we are disappointed and convey that disappointment to our kids. One pediatrician says, "[Children] are in a sphincter-tightening, teeth-grinding kind of environment. You see them in class and their mouths are twisted, their tongues are out, they're sweating a little."[5] These unmet expectations become a problem both for parents and for their children.[6]

## Gradual Departure

One Sunday after church I was standing in our main hallway watching our oldest daughter interact with some other children. I suppose the expression on my face betrayed my deep feelings of love for Julia. As I stood there gazing at my seven-year-old, an older dad said, "Robert, some day that girl of yours is going to break your heart." At first, the comment caught me off guard. I didn't know if he was predicting some act of rebellion or moral lapse that would disappoint me. Frankly, I resented his comment.

But last Saturday, I began to understand what he meant. A few weeks ago, I had decided that Julia and I were not spending enough time together. So I had an idea. I was going to drive to Ft. Worth the next week for a television interview and thought Julia might like to spend the entire day with me. After the interview, we would go to the movie (something we both have always enjoyed), play miniature golf, and do whatever she would like to do. Initially, she was excited by the idea.

But last Saturday, as we were driving together to McDonalds, I could tell something was troubling her.

"What's wrong, Julia?"

"Dad, there's something I need to tell you. But I'm afraid I'll hurt your feelings."

"What is it, Sweetheart?"

"You know that trip we were going to take together next Friday?"

"Yes."

"Well, next Friday after school, Lauren is having a special birthday party. A trolley is going to come by our house to pick me up. And all my friends are going to be there. I would really like to go, but I don't want to hurt your feelings."

At that moment, I understand exactly what my older parishioner was trying to communicate to me. Ken Davis has written,

The moment the doctor cuts the umbilical cord, kids begin a mad dash for freedom. They don't make much headway at first, because they can't communicate real well. . . . This drive for independence intensifies as kids approach adolescence and struggle to control their own lives. It can be a confusing and difficult time for a parent—the child who has always been compliant and obedient is suddenly fighting you at every turn. The little kid who needed you so desperately for so many years, the one who clung to your leg like a growth, now prefers to be on his own.[7]

Although our children's move toward independence is part of God's natural order, it can also be a troubling experience for fathers and just one more source of discontent for a man involved in a mid-life reevaluation.

## THE GIFT OF PARENTING

Inadequate time, insufficient money, unmet expectations, and the gradual departure of our children cannot be avoided. But they need not rob fathers of contentment. Let's look at five principles that will help us see our parenting responsibilities from God's perspective.

### View Your Children as a Gift from God

The psalmist declared, "Behold, children are a gift of the LORD" (Ps. 127:3). Many Old Testament commentators point out that the word translated *gift* could also be translated *inheritance*. It is a Hebrew word that was used to describe the promised land which God gave to the Israelites. Our children should be thought of as an undeserved inheritance from our heavenly Father.

Whenever we think of an inheritance, we think of a sum of money left to us by a loved one that is free of any strings and, therefore, available to spend as we please. After all, if poor Uncle

Billy is six feet under, how will he know (and why would he care) if we buy a Lamborghini with the loot he left? It's *our* money.

But unlike Uncle Billy, God is not dead, and He is *very* interested in what we do with the gifts He bestows upon us. Perhaps this illustration will help. About five years ago, my grandfather called his grandchildren together and presented each one of us with a check. But there were conditions attached to the gift. "I expect you to triple this money in your lifetime. You are free to spend the interest as you choose, but I want you to keep the principal safe. If an emergency arises and I need the money back some day, I expect you to return it without any whining."

Were we happy to receive the gift? We were elated. Never before had we held so much money in our hands. But that excitement was tempered by the realization that we were responsible to care for and maximize our grandfather's gift.

In the same way, the psalmist says that we should view our children as an undeserved gift from God. But we need to understand what kind of gift our children are:

*Our children are a gift of real value.* About the same time my grandfather gave us the money, another relative died and left us a "gift": some worn-out lawn furniture that is sitting in our garage. While I spend time each week thinking about ways to invest and multiply my grandfather's gift, I don't think too much about that lawn furniture. The wood is rotting, the metal is rusting—any attempt to restore it would not be worth the effort. It is a gift of no value.

How do you view your children? Do you treat them like a large sum of money or a piece of rusty lawn furniture? We need to understand that our children are gifts of incredible value that deserve our attention.

*Our children are a temporary gift.* Last month I performed the funeral service for a teenager who was gunned down in an act of senseless violence. The teenage boy had accompanied his father on a business trip to Atlanta. For several years they had been estranged from one another, but God was healing their relationship. The trip would afford them the opportunity to spend some quality time together. That night in the motel room, the boy and father made plans what they were going to do the next day. The boy then asked his dad if it would be all right if he left the motel room to call his girlfriend from the pay phone across the street. While on the phone to his girlfriend, a gang approached the phone booth and shot the boy to death.

The father, alarmed by his son's prolonged absence and the sound of sirens, left his motel room to search for his son. As he saw the crowd forming around the pay phone, the father knew something was horribly wrong. As he pressed his way through the crowd, the father discovered the almost lifeless body of his son, his life's blood being pumped onto the concrete pavement. Cradling the head of his dying son in his lap as he waited for the ambulance, the father repeated over and over again, "I love you, Son; I love you."

Summoning his last breath, the son said, "I love you, too, Dad," and with those final words the boy slipped into eternity. Suddenly. without any warning, their nineteen-year relationship was over. Never again—at least in this life—would they talk, argue, or laugh with one another.

As I shared that final scene with those present at the funeral service, I knew that every father present was going to return home and hug his children that night.

Yes, our children can be taken from us prematurely. But even if we never experience a tragedy, we should remember that our time with our children is still severely limited. Before we know it, they will depart our homes to begin their own. Author Tim Hansel claims that if you are 35 and live until 70, you really only have 500 days left to live, after taking care of necessities like working, eating, and sleeping. "When I put life in that context, it helps me realize that I am a father for so short a time, I dare not take it for granted."[8]

*Our children are a gift for which we are accountable.* Do you remember Jesus' parable about the talents? A master who was departing on a long journey called his slaves together and entrusted his possessions to them. One slave was given five talents; another, two; and still another was given only one. The three slaves understood that the master would return one day and ask for his money back. Until that day, they were to care for and multiply their master's assets. Jesus said, "Now after a long time the master of those slaves came and settled accounts with them" (Matt. 25:19).

The point of the parable is about as subtle as a battering ram. Jesus is warning us that one day He will ask us to account for all the gifts He has given to us: money, abilities, time, positions . . . and our children.

- Have we imparted to our children the skills they need to live successfully?
- Have we given them the self-confidence they need to face life's difficulties?
- Have we communicated to them that there is at least one person who loves them unconditionally?
- Have we taught and modeled for them that the most important thing in life is to love and obey God?

To see God's plan in our children, we must first view our children the way God views them—as valuable gifts that are to be treasured.

## Value Your Child's Uniqueness

The same God who built your wife also oversaw the intricate and unique design of your children. Nothing was left to chance. Let's go back to Psalm 139 for a moment: "For thou didst form _____'s (now insert your child's name) inward parts; Thou didst weave [him/her] in [his/her] mother's womb" (v. 13).

I want you to note two key words in this verse. The first is translated *inward parts*. The Hebrew word literally means "kidneys" and is representative of all of the internal organs of the embryo. But I believe the word refers to more than kidneys, livers, hearts, and brains. I believe the word also describes the disposition, the interests, the abilities, and even the tendencies toward sin in our child. (Remember Ps. 51:5: "Behold, I was brought forth in iniquity, and in sin my mother conceived me"? Our sin nature was not learned; it was inherited in the womb.)

The second important word here is *weave*. The word is used in Hebrew literature to describe the interweaving of a large vine. God has woven together all our children's physical, emotional, and spiritual characteristics into one complex creation.

What does this brief lesson in Hebrew have to do with contentment? Your child is God's unique creation. Appreciate—yes, even celebrate—the fact that there is not another child like yours anywhere. Chuck Swindoll takes this important truth and applies it to where we live:

> Some kids are made for the ballet floor. Some are made for a violin. Some are made to play a horn. Some are made to paint. Some are made to dribble a ball all over the court, jump like crazy, and stuff that round pill into the hoop. Some are made for the gridiron—they're linebackers. But don't try to make a linebacker into a ballet dancer. Can you imagine a guy like Bosworth or Butkus on a ballet floor? Can you imagine Baryshnikov as a tight end for the Chicago Bears? Get serious.[9]

### Be Willing to Sacrifice for Your Children

When I was a youth minister I would often ask teenagers what topic they would like the speaker at our youth camp to address. "Dating" was always the hands-down favorite. But the second most requested topic was "How can I know God's will for my life?"

I don't think teenagers are the only ones interested in that subject. If I claim to love God, it is natural that I would want to know His plan for my life. But contrary to popular opinion, God's will is not some mystery that has to be discovered by reading tea leaves or by analyzing obscure Greek and Hebrew words. God's will for your life is clearly spelled out in the Bible: "For whom He foreknew, He also predestined to become conformed to the image of His Son, that He might be the first-born among many brethren" (Rom. 8:29).

Since this is not a doctrinal book, let's lay aside the thorny issue of predestination and concentrate on the ultimate purpose for which we have been predestined: "to become conformed to the image of His Son." God's will for your life is simple: He wants you to become just like Jesus Christ in your attitudes, your actions, and your affections. God wants you to think like Jesus thought, love what Jesus loved, and behave like Jesus would behave in every situation. How does God make you like Christ?

I've devoted an entire book to answering that question (*Heaven Can't Wait,* Broadman & Holman Publishers). But let's just look at one character quality God wants to develop in our lives so that we can be like Christ: unselfishness.

I think you will agree that Jesus Christ was more concerned with others than He was with Himself. Two Scripture passages come to mind:

> "Just as the Son of Man did not come to be served, but to serve, and to give His life a ransom for many." (Matt. 20:28)
>
> Do nothing from selfishness or empty conceit, but with humility of mind let each of you regard one another as more important than himself; do not merely look out for your own personal interests, but also for the interests of others. Have this attitude in yourselves which was also in Christ Jesus. (Phil. 2:3–5)

If God's will for my life is that I resemble Jesus Christ in my attitudes, actions, and affections, that means God wants me to be unselfish like His Son. How does God teach me to

- be more interested in serving than in being served?
- regard others as more important than myself?
- look out for others' needs before my own?

One way God accomplishes that is by giving us children. Being a father encourages you to put the needs of others above your own. Author Steve Farrar use this scenario to illustrate that truth:

You'll find yourself in the bathroom at two in the morning with the shower going full blast. You, however, won't be in the shower. You'll be sitting on the toilet seat holding your little girl who has the croup, since the only thing that will break it up is plenty of hot steam. I doubt that's what you'd normally choose to do at that time of night. But you have as much love in your heart for your little girl as she has congestion in her lungs. So you sit there and love her and try to remember what it was like to sleep eight hours straight.[10]

Let me mention two specific sacrifices that every father must learn to make for his children:

*Money.* One dad was explaining to a friend why he was driving an old car that had the bumper wired to the front of it. "I have to admit it's embarrassing to drive a car that's literally falling apart, but I've got a good reason. My wife and I are committed to staying out of debt so we don't financially strangle our family. We want to have fun family experiences. We want to travel together. We want to send our kids to Christian camps. If we drove a late-model car, we couldn't afford those things. So we made our choice."[11]

What financial sacrifices are *you* willing to make for the welfare of your children?:

- Are you willing to give up an expensive hobby so that your children can attend an athletic camp this summer?
- Are you willing to drive an older car so that your teenagers might have a car they're not embarrassed to be seen in?
- Are you willing to postpone your retirement so that you can generate enough income to finance their education?
- Are you willing to give up that new suit so that your two girls might have new Easter dresses this year (my wife must have slipped this one in)?

*Time.* Some fathers find it easier to relinquish money than to sacrifice another sacred commodity: time. Our children need us to spend time—lots of time—with them. And that is not always easy. When I come home from work each evening, I am absolutely drained. All I want to do is open my paper, turn on the news, and vegetate a few minutes before supper. But my children have a different idea. There is nothing in the world my three-year-old enjoys more than my pushing her on her swing set. She isn't content with just a few minutes of swinging. She would love for me to spend hours pushing her and singing to her. She doesn't really understand why I go to work every day. She is unaware of the money I am setting aside for her college education. She isn't that impressed with the gifts I give her—a bag of M&Ms is just as popular as a new tricycle. But it is those hours spent swinging her that best communicate my love for her.

That time invested with my daughter instead of with my newspaper and that money spent on Easter dresses instead of a new suit are contributing to an even greater purpose: my becoming more like Jesus Christ. How can you find contentment with the numerous sacrifices you must make as a father? By understanding that those sacrifices are not obstacles on your road to happiness, but they are the means by which you discover God's true purpose for your life.

I began the chapter by talking about the incredible balancing act fathers must perform. At times the pressure can be unbearable. Who among us has never thought—even for an instant—of running away and starting over again. But I believe that fatherhood also offers us the opportunity to fulfill one of the greatest needs all men have: to make an impact on the world that is felt long after we are gone. Rabbi Harold Kushner once said there are three things every man should do before he dies: plant a tree, write a book, and have a child. Why? A tree, a book, and a child will live beyond our death. Eventually trees die and books go out of print. But through our children—and our children's children—our influence will be felt for generations to come.

## FOR FURTHER REFLECTION

1. Which of the "balancing acts" is causing you the most difficulty now? Why?

2. List your three greatest expectations for each of your children. What is the source of those expectations: your desires, your child's gifts and interests, or timeless principles from God's Word?

CHILD'S NAME     MY EXPECTATION     SOURCE OF EXPECTATION

3. As you consider the limited amount of time you have to spend with your child, what changes do you need to make in your life?

4. List five qualities you appreciate most about each of your children. Make a special appointment with them this week (maybe for dinner or just an ice cream cone) to share your list with them.

5. What are some practical sacrifices you could make this month for the well-being of your children?

# CHAPTER EIGHT

## Seeing God's Hand in the Hurts of Others

s I write these words, our entire nation is reeling from the shock of the bombing of the Alfred P. Murrah Federal building in Oklahoma City. I realize by the time you read these words, almost a year will have passed since that horrible event on April 19, 1995. The suspects probably will have been apprehended and perhaps a verdict will have been reached. More than likely, another tragedy will have captured the country's attention. But few of us will forget the powerful images burned into our consciousness via the media: a fireman holding the limp, unrecognizable body of a bloodied infant, rescue workers crawling through the rubble of the building searching for any signs of life, a suspect being escorted in chains through an angry crowd yelling "Baby killer!"

But the picture I will always remember will be that of a police car patrolling the almost deserted streets of Oklahoma City with these words written in shoe polish across the back window: "WE WILL NEVER FORGET." The outrage over such a senseless act of violence is understandable. The resolve to never forget the victims is admirable. But the unwillingness to let go of bitterness can be just as damaging as the blast of any bomb.

I've wondered why those words on the police car made such an impression on me. I suppose it is because I've heard those words or sentiments expressed too many times.

- A husband who discovers that his wife of twenty-five years has been having an affair with his best friend . . . I WILL NEVER FORGET.
- A hard-working employee who was summarily dismissed because of office politics . . . I WILL NEVER FORGET.
- A church member who was ridiculed in a business meeting by the pastor . . . I WILL NEVER FORGET.
- A businessman who loses a career-breaking deal to a competitor who slandered him to get the business . . . I WILL NEVER FORGET.
- A father who listens to his twenty-three-year-old daughter spew forth all kinds of accusations of neglect and emotional abuse and admit that she has never really loved her dad . . . I WILL NEVER FORGET.

Too many times that refrain is looked upon as evidence of great emotional strength. Bitterness and revenge are to be admired. Only doormats and Casper Milquetoasts allow themselves to be walked all over by others. I read in *Newsweek* magazine recently about a famous executive known for his ruthless ways and his resolve to always get even. His goal? "I want everyone in this industry to know that they had better not ——— with me." Let's admit it. All of us secretly admire someone like that. We all wish we could generate enough fear in others that they wouldn't mess with us. And we mistakenly believe that the best way to engender that respect is to avenge any and every wrong inflicted upon us. Sometimes we feel as if hate is the only real power that we possess.

Lewis Smedes recounts the experience of Mark and Karen Zwaak. Karen was an aggressive, domineering wife who couldn't understand why her husband was no stronger than he was. She constantly ridiculed him in front of their friends for his inability to make decisions, get a raise, or confront the mechanic who ripped him off. After one particular humiliating attack by his wife in the presence of some friends, Mark exploded. On the way home from the party, Mark screamed, "For this, I will never forgive you, never!" And he made good on his pledge. Then Smedes makes this profound observation: "His hate became his secret pet; he succored it, nourished it, fondled it, and let it roam the ranges of his soul. His hate felt to him like a generator of inner power. But his hate was only surface strength. Beneath his hate, he still suspected that Karen had him sized up right; he really was weak, impotent, ineffective. His hate was a cover for the weakness he dared not face."[1]

The "road most traveled" includes deep wounds inflicted by spouses, parents, bosses, pastors, or children. When a man reaches the years of the mid-life evaluation, he is often carrying with him the emotional baggage of years of hostility or bitterness toward those who have wronged him. To ask a man to let go of those offenses is like asking him to surrender the only weapon he has left to deal with his hurt. Yet I am convinced that the single most important decision you can make—outside of your decision to become a Christian—is the decision to forgive those who have offended you. Forgiveness is a key to your physical, emotional, and spiritual wholeness.

I recently asked our media department what sermon tapes generated the most response. Among the top sellers were messages about marriage, parenting, and Bible prophecy. But the best-selling tapes by far were those that dealt with the subjects of worry and forgiveness. Many times when I speak on the subject of forgiveness I ask the audience to recall the name of someone who has hurt them deeply in the past and to briefly relive that hurtful experience. I explain that to be able to apply the truths about forgiveness, we first of all have to have someone to forgive. Forgiveness must have an object. Then, about thirty seconds later, I ask everyone who has a person in mind to raise their hand. There is always a unanimous response. *All* of us have been hurt by someone, somewhere, at some time.

In fact, to make this chapter relevant to you, I would suggest that you take a moment to recall someone who has hurt you in the past.

The Person: _____

The Offense: _____

Did it amaze you how quickly you were able to recall the person and the offense? My purpose in writing this chapter is to do more than impart to you a lot of information, illustrations, and insights about forgiveness. Ultimately, I want you to be able to let go of the above hurt you have experienced. There is probably little you could have done to have prevented the experience. Rarely can we control what circumstances or other people do to us. But we *can* control how we respond to those circumstances and hurts. As you go through a mid-life reevaluation, one of the most important "course corrections" you can make is the decision to confront and forgive the hurts inflicted by others. In this chapter we will learn how and why we must forgive.

## "MY GOD, MY GOD, WHY . . ."

Bob and Cathy came to talk with me last week after attending our service the previous Sunday. Bob was a member of another church who had recently felt the stirrings of spiritual renewal in his life and desired to go deeper in his faith. Cathy was Jewish and was interested in becoming a Christian. But she had many questions. How could she know for sure that Jesus was the Messiah? Could she keep her Jewish traditions and still be a Christian? Would God send her parents, along with all Jews and non-Christians, to hell? Typical questions that received typical, evangelical responses.

But I could tell Cathy was saving the "biggie" for last. "If there really is a God, why does He allow so much suffering in the world?" Good question. In fact, I thought about her question this week as I read about a family in Los Angeles murdered "execution style" in front of two children. First the killers shot the father in the head, then the mother, then the five-year-old son, and finally the six-month-old boy as the two surviving children watched. Why would a loving God allow such an atrocity?

Why would a loving God allow you to suffer the hurt you have experienced? If there really is a God who is supposedly running the universe, why would He allow . . .

- a jealous coworker's lie to cost you your job?
- a dishonest broker to cheat you out of your retirement savings?
- an adulterous wife to destroy your family?
- a drunk driver to kill your son in a head-on collision?

## Why Ask Why?

It would be presumptuous to try to solve the problem of evil in three pages. Theologians have wrestled with the question for centuries. Yet I do believe the Bible gives some insights about why God allows His children to experience pain.

*The hurts of others are the result of living in a fallen world.* The third chapter of Genesis is not just an interesting story about a serpent, a woman, and a piece of fruit. Moses wanted us to understand how evil corrupted the beautiful world God had created. Because of Adam's and Eve's transgression, sin has infected every part of our lives. Sin's influence is not partial, but total. Perhaps this illustration will help.

My father taught me many things before he died, including how to make the world's best homemade vanilla ice cream. One thing he always warned me about was allowing any of the rock salt into the mixture. On one occasion I wasn't careful enough and a few particles of salt found their way into the ice cream. Not realizing what had happened, I proudly dished out my creation to each of the family members. We all took the first bite and—in unison— gagged. Several minute particles of salt had ruined the entire batch of ice cream. And everyone suffered for it!

It is the same way with sin. The fall resulted in sin flavoring every aspect of our existence. Everything wrong in our world today—from broken radiator hoses to broken relationships—can ultimately be traced back to living in a sin-infected world. That is why Paul wrote, "For the anxious longing of the creation waits eagerly for the revealing of the sons of God. For the creation was subjected to futility, not of its own will . . . in hope that the creation itself also will be set free from its slavery to corruption" (Rom. 8:19–21). Paul says that only when Christ returns will the effects of sin be overturned.

*The hurts of others cause us to be more like Christ.* Frankly, it is of little comfort to know that the only explanation for the problems others are inflicting upon us is something that happened thousands of years ago in a remote garden, halfway around the world. Has God removed His hand from the world—or more importantly, from my life—until Christ returns to redeem the earth? Am I just a helpless victim in this world of violence and heartache? Are other people free agents who may choose to hurt me in any way they determine? No, God can use the injustices others commit against us to achieve His purpose in our life.

God's number one purpose for your life is to make you like Jesus Christ. Exactly how is God going to accomplish that? Maybe you have traveled to Italy and seen Michaelangelo's fabulous sculpture of David. One can only imagine the hours spent carefully chiseling away at that piece of marble to create that magnificent work of art.

Picture yourself as a giant slab of marble from which God wants to create the exact image of His Son. How does He do it? God must "chisel" away the imperfections of your life. We said in the last chapter that if we are to resemble Jesus Christ, God must chisel away our propensity to selfishness. One way He does that is by giving us a family to care for.

To be like Christ, we must also learn to forgive others as Christ did. The apostle Peter was an eyewitness to Jesus' response to mistreatment. "And while being reviled, He did not revile in return; while suffering, He uttered no threats, but kept entrusting

Himself to Him who judges righteously" (1 Pet. 2:23). "Oh, wasn't Jesus a nice person" you say. But Peter had a reason for telling us this. "Christ also suffered for *you,* leaving *you* an example for *you* to follow in His steps" (1 Pet. 2:21, emphasis mine).

God wants us to demonstrate the same ability to forgive our offenders and entrust them to God that Christ had. But how can we learn to do that if we are never hurt by another person? The offenses of others are just some of the "blows" God uses to shape us into the image of His Son.

*The hurts of others allow us to minister to other people.* Have you ever wondered why God created you? "To have fellowship with Him" you correctly answer. If that's true, then why does God *leave* you on this planet after you become a Christian—why not an immediate express trip to heaven? Couldn't you enjoy a more perfect relationship with God in heaven? I am convinced that the primary reason God leaves His children on earth is for the purpose of ministry. Isn't that what the Great Commission is all about: introducing unbelievers to Christ and helping believers grow in their relationship with God?

When you view your life through the lens of ministry, it gives you a different perspective on all your life circumstances—including the hurts of others. God can use the wrong attitudes and actions of others to further His purpose.

Let's return to Paul for a moment as he was under house arrest in Rome. Some of Paul's enemies were gloating over his imprisonment. "You need to listen to us instead of to Paul. If he were really God's servant, he wouldn't be in prison." Paul had every reason to be embittered against these so-called preachers of the gospel. But what was his response? "In every way, whether in pretense or in truth, Christ is proclaimed; and in this I rejoice" (Phil. 1:18). Paul was able to see how the wrongs of others could advance the cause of Christ. And since that was his ultimate goal in life, why should he be upset?

In the same way, God can use the hurts of others in your life to further His kingdom. For example, maybe you have gone through a painful divorce. You tried every way imaginable to keep your wife from leaving you, but the lure of another man was too powerful for her to resist. The sting of your hurt and humiliation is acute, even after several years. Nevertheless, God has given you the strength to go on—one day at a time. One day a coworker confides to you that his wife is in the process of leaving him. He doesn't know what to do. You sense his despair and share with him how God has helped you. No, he doesn't bow his head and pray the sinner's prayer and walk down the aisle of your church the next week. But you have ministered to him. His curiosity is piqued. You have begun a dialogue that might indeed lead to his salvation.

Too idealistic, you say? Not really. Paul described how God can use our hurts as ministry opportunities: "Blessed be . . . the God of all comfort, who comforts us in all our affliction so that we may be able to comfort those who are in any affliction with the comfort with which we ourselves are comforted by God" (2 Cor. 1:3–4).

*The hurts of others can give us direction in life.* God's ultimate will for our lives is that we become like Jesus Christ in our actions, attitudes, and affections. But I also believe that God has a detailed plan for our lives that encompasses everything from the choice of our spouse to the choice of our vocation. How does God communicate His plan to us and how does He actually place us where He wants us to be? Many times it is through the hurts of other people. Consider the story of Jacob.

Jacob had worked for his uncle Laban for twenty years. Although it had been a volatile partnership, Jacob had become comfortable with the arrangement. But God had a different plan for Jacob. It was time for him to move back to Canaan. How did God communicate to Jacob that it was time to move? The Bible says that "Jacob saw the attitude of Laban, and behold, it was not friendly toward him as formerly" (Gen. 31:2). Apparently, Laban had become hostile toward Jacob and had cheated him out of some money.

It would have been natural for Jacob to have responded with hurt or outrage over Laban's mistreatment. "Look at all I've done for you—tending to these stinking sheep for twenty years. And this is the thanks I get." But notice what Jacob said to his wives: "I see your father's attitude, that is not friendly toward me as formerly, but the God of my father has been with me. And you know that I have served your father with all my strength. Yet your father has cheated me and changed my wages ten times; however, God did not allow him to hurt me" (Gen. 31:5–7).

Jacob believed in a God who was powerful enough to work through Laban's mistreatment. And it was that faith that kept Jacob from being paralyzed with bitterness. Regardless of Laban's motives, God was still working out His plan for Jacob's life. God used Laban's offense to move Jacob back to Canaan. In the same way, God can use the offenses of your employer, your spouse, or your children to accomplish His purpose for your life.

Understanding the reasons that God allows others to hurt us is not enough to motivate us to forgive. I think of the example of Simon Wiesenthal, a Jewish prisoner in a Polish concentration camp. One day Wiesenthal was assigned to clean out the garbage from a hospital the Germans were using to care for injured soldiers from the Eastern Front. A nurse appeared and asked Wiesenthal to accompany her. In a few moments he found himself in the presence of an SS Trooper. The soldier grasped Wiesenthal's hand and explained that he had to talk to a Jew before he died. The trooper felt the need to confess the atrocities he had committed and to know he had been forgiven before he met his Maker. So he began to spill out his sin.

He had been fighting in a Russian village where two hundred Jews were captured. His group was ordered to plant cans of gasoline in a particular house. Then the soldiers marched those two hundred Jews in the house. They were packed so tightly that they could barely move. The soldiers threw grenades through the windows to set the house on fire and were ordered to shoot anyone who tried to jump out of the window. The SS Trooper remembered, "Behind the window of the second floor, I saw a man with a small child in his arms. His clothing was alight. By his side stood a woman, doubtless the mother of the child. With his free hand the man covered the child's eyes—then he jumped into the street.

Seconds later, the mother followed. We shot . . . Oh, God . . . I shall never forget it—it haunts me."

The soldier then said, "I know what I have told you is terrible. I have longed to talk about it to a Jew and beg forgiveness from him. I know that what I am asking is almost too much, but without your answer I cannot die in peace."

Wiesenthal later wrote, "I stood up and looked in his direction, at his folded hands. At last I made up my mind and without a word I left the room."[2] Simon Wiesenthal made a choice. I WILL NEVER FORGET. I WILL NOT FORGIVE.

## THE SUPERNATURAL BENEFITS OF FORGIVENESS

I cannot be too hard on Simon Wiesenthal. If I were in his situation, I cannot be sure what I would have done—and neither can you. But I do know that had I chosen not to forgive that soldier, I would have lost as much as he. Forgiveness benefits us as much as it does our enemy. How?

### Forgiveness Produces Physical Wholeness

The relationship between unresolved anger toward others (or ourselves, as we will discuss in the next chapter) is well documented. Anger decreases the lymphocytes in our bodies, which results in decreased antibodies needed to fight infectious diseases. Christian psychiatrists Frank Minirth and Paul Meier claim "Pent-up anger is probably the leading cause of death."[3] Bitterness is a deadly toxin that poisons our bodies.

One writer relates the story of a pastor's wife who had cancer. The couple sought the best medical care available. The physician they selected had been studying the relationship between cancer and negative emotions, and began counseling with the wife. For weeks he asked her about any unresolved conflict she had with others. He tried his best to get her to open up and to cry, but she wouldn't respond.

One day, in the midst of their conversation, she began to weep uncontrollably. She admitted the bitterness she had felt toward her parents for many years. Immediately she was freed from the bitterness that had held her hostage for so long. Today, the writer says, she is alive and active in ministry. The doctor is convinced she would have never recovered had she not dealt with her bitterness.[4]

One of the most powerful testimonials about the relationship between forgiveness and healing comes from a daughter who did not always agree with her dad, but learned by his example some of life's most important lessons. The daughter is Patti Davis. The father is former President Ronald Reagan. In her book *Angels Don't Die: My Father's Gift of Faith,* she relates the story of her father's recovery after being gunned down by assassin John Hinckley:

> [My father] said he knew that his physical healing was directly dependent on his ability to forgive John Hinckley. Forgiveness is hard work, but my father made it sound effortless.
>
> Many times I'd listened to my father tell me that we are all God's children. Maybe at one time I chalked it up to the language of a churchgoing man. But when he referred to John Hinckley as "misguided," I felt the weight of that word—the weight of what it said about my father. He never expressed hatred for the man who had shot him. He expressed pity. He knew in his world that even Hinckley belonged to God. That knowledge leads to forgiveness; it transforms and heals.[5]

### Forgiveness Produces Emotional Freedom

A number of years ago, a friend invited me to invest in a business venture with him. The deal had the promise of a large return. Not knowing much about this particular business and trusting my friend, I invested a substantial amount of cash with him. The arrangement was simple. I would provide the cash, he would provide the sweat. Unfortunately, the deal did not work out, and my friend promised to return my money. Weeks went by and there was no check. I began calling my friend daily, and he would assure me that I would have the money by the end of the week. Still nothing. I would stop by his office and ask for the money. Still no response. Every time I saw him, all I could think about was the money he owed me. After many months of emotional turmoil, I concluded I was never going to see my money again. In my mind, I canceled the debt he owed me. I was emotionally free. I quit calling. I stopped going by his office. It was over.

Now, let's make the obvious analogy. When someone hurts you, they become indebted to you. They have caused an injury that has produced an emotional debt. They "owe" you—at least in your mind—for what they have done to you. Their offense is like an account receivable you are holding. As long as you keep holding on to that debt, you are in emotional bondage to that individual. "When are they going to realize how much they have hurt me? When are they going to ask for forgiveness?" But when you forgive that person, you are unilaterally and unconditionally releasing them from their debt. And you can be emotionally free.

I have counseled a number of people who have asked, "Why should I forgive _____ , unless he/she asks for (or earns) my forgiveness?" To make forgiveness dependent on what your offender does (or doesn't do) is to make you an emotional slave to that individual. Why would you want to tie your emotional well-being to an individual? I believe the Bible teaches that we are not to be emotional slaves to any person. "Owe nothing to anyone except to love one another" (Rom. 13:8). When I forgive another person, I am canceling the debt he owes me so that I might be set free to love God and to serve others.

## Forgiveness Produces Spiritual Freedom

Isaiah the prophet wrote, "But your iniquities have made a separation between you and your God" (59:2). Most of us tend to relate that verse to salvation. "Sin is a wall between God and us that Jesus Christ abolished through His death on the cross" we explain. And that is certainly true.

But I believe the verse has application to Christians as well. Our sin—whether it be immorality, greed, or bitterness—can separate us from God *after* we become Christians. No, God does not revoke our salvation. But these sins have a way of muting God's voice in our lives. Immorality, greed, and bitterness are cruel taskmasters that demand all of our attention. I cannot be focused on serving God if I am focused on my next sexual conquest, or on my stock portfolio, or on the person who has wronged me. (Perhaps that is why Jesus said it is impossible to serve God and money.)

George was a deacon in a former church who had experienced a run-in with my predecessor. When I came to pastor the church, George was one of the first people to invite me to lunch. Without many preliminaries, he began to tell me how the previous pastor had hurt him. George's hatred for the former pastor had long since quenched his interest in reading the Bible or praying. George could not listen to my sermons without thinking of my predecessor. "When _____ preached that passage, he would say . . ." George's bitterness had become a barrier that kept him from being able to hear the voice of God.

Is there some hurt from your past that has absorbed your emotional and spiritual energy? Letting go of the hurt will demolish that wall between you and God and will free you to once again experience intimacy with Him.

## LETTING GO

"All right," you say, "I know I *need* to forgive, but *how* do I do it?" Glad you asked! Allow me to share with you four invaluable keys to letting go of those hurts that are hindering your physical, emotional, and spiritual wholeness.

### Admit That You Have Been Hurt

Remember that the word *forgiveness* relates to the releasing of a debt. When another person hurts us, we feel they "owe" us for that hurt. As long as we refuse to forgive that person, we are carrying around an "account receivable" in our minds that keeps us in emotional bondage to that person. But if we never admit that we have been hurt, then there is no debt to forgive. "What's the problem with that?" you ask. Isn't it better to overlook the offenses of others to begin with than to carry around this emotional debt? If we were perfect, perhaps that would be true, but consider this illustration.

Let's say you are parked at a red light and *bam!*—someone rear-ends you. Startled, you get out of the car, walk around the back to inspect the damage. Amazingly, nothing seems to be wrong. The driver apologizes profusely, offering to give you his business card and the name of his insurance agent. Feeling magnanimous, you tell him, "No problem," and drive off. You have overlooked his transgression.

The next day you begin to notice a strange rattle in the rear end of your car and feel your car pulling strongly to the right. You take the car to your mechanic and discover that yesterday's accident did indeed cause some damage to your car—about $500 worth. Who's going to pay for the repairs? *You* are because you prematurely let the other guy off the hook. And you feel like the world's biggest jerk.

Now let's rewind this little drama to the part where you are getting out of the car to inspect the damage. In this version of the story, you look at your car and there is a huge dent in the bumper. You know it is going to be expensive to repair. But this time the driver is a little old lady who is in tears over the accident. Between sobs she explains that she is a retired missionary who has no insurance and no money. "What am I going to do?" she laments. You tell her to forget it, you will take care of the damage. The next day you take the car to the dealership and discover that the car will cost $500 to repair. Although you are perturbed at first about shelling out that kind of money, you remember that woman's look of relief when you told her not to worry about it.

Do you feel like an idiot this time? No, because you *consciously* chose to forgive her of a large debt. It would be great if we could instantly overlook the hurts of others. But offenses are like the mysterious rattles in a car—they will stay with us unless we decisively deal with them.

One of the greatest myths about forgiveness is that "time heals." "If you will just forget about what that other person did, then time will take care of your hurt." Think for just a minute about how silly that comment is. Imagine that you go to a dentist and he discovers you have a large cavity. Would he say, "Don't worry about that hole in your tooth. Time will heal it"? Or suppose your doctor delivers the news that he has discovered a malignancy in your liver. "But don't worry," he advises. "Time heals."

Our neighbors have a large tree right next to our driveway. The tree's root is expanding underneath the concrete, causing it to buckle and to crack. Eventually, something is going to have to been done to that root before it ruins our driveway. The longer I ignore the problem, the more costly the damage will be. The Bible teaches that bitterness is like rotting decay, or a spreading malignancy, or an expanding root that must be cut out of our lives. "See to it that no one comes short of the grace of God; that no root of bitterness springing up causes trouble, and by it many be defiled" (Heb. 12:15). But in order to deal decisively with that root of bitterness, we must first acknowledge that another person has offended us.

### Recognize Your Own Need for Forgiveness

To me, this is the most important step in the process of forgiveness. Before we can release someone else of their debt, we must first realize the tremendous debt from which God has released us. Jesus told a fascinating story to illustrate that truth (see Matt. 18:23–35). I like to call it "The Tale of Two Debtors." One day a king decided to call in all of his accounts receivable. One of the king's debtors was a slave who owed the king 10,000 talents. A talent was approximately 60–80 pounds of gold or silver. If Jesus was referring to gold, that would mean that the slave owed the king about five billion dollars! When the king asked for his money back, the slave begged for mercy, offering to pay back everything he owed—an impossibility considering the size of his debt. But the king "felt compassion and released him and forgave him the debt." Can you imagine the relief the slave felt?

But here's the interesting twist to the story. This slave also happened to be a lender himself. A fellow slave owed him a debt of one hundred denarii, or about $16. The slave who had just been forgiven the multi-billion-dollar debt demanded his $16 back. The fellow slave begged for compassion, but the first slave offered none. He had his fellow slave thrown into prison until the paltry sum was repaid.

When the king heard this story, he was infuriated. How could a man who had been forgiven of so much refuse to forgive so little a debt? The king was so angry that he had the first slave arrested and turned over to the "torturers" until he repaid his five-billion-dollar debt.

Now, if you haven't gotten the point by this time, Jesus adds the zinger. "So shall My heavenly Father also do to you, if each of you does not forgive his brother from your heart" (Matt. 18:35). Jesus is saying that, in light of the tremendous debt that God has forgiven us, we should be willing to forgive others. The difference between our offenses against God and others' offenses against us is the difference between $5 billion and $16. The betrayal of a friend, the dishonesty of a business partner, or the unfaithfulness of a spouse are very real hurts that must be acknowledged. But before you decide "I will never forget," consider what God has chosen to forget about you. Take a stroll down memory lane and relive some of the sins you have committed—sins that you hope to heaven no one ever finds out. When you remember those transgressions that were committed against a holy God who, unlike us, has a zero tolerance level for sin, aren't you grateful that He chose to forgive you? Considering the tremendous debt from which you have been released, shouldn't you be able to release that friend, or partner, or spouse?

In Matthew 6:14 Jesus said, "For if you forgive men for their transgressions, your heavenly Father will also forgive you. But if you do not forgive men, then your Father will not forgive your transgressions." Many people have been confused by this verse. Do I earn God's forgiveness by forgiving others? Can I lose God's forgiveness if I choose not to forgive another? No, I believe Jesus is saying that our willingness to forgive others is the *evidence* that God has forgiven us. But if we find it impossible to forgive another person it may be because we have never experienced God's forgiveness ourselves. To try to forgive another person without first having experienced God's forgiveness is like writing a check on an empty bank account. You do not possess the resources necessary to make the transaction. Only when your heart is full of gratitude for God's forgiveness of your offenses will you ever find it possible to forgive others. That is why Paul said, "Be kind to one another, tender-hearted, forgiving each other, just as God in Christ also has forgiven you" (Eph. 4:32).

### "Stake Down" the Time and Place of Your Forgiveness

Many times I counsel people who say "I cannot remember when or if I ever became a Christian, and the doubt has been plaguing me for years." I always say to a person in that situation "It is often too difficult to remember what we did many years ago, especially when we were children. But regardless of what you did or did not do in the past, why don't you pray with me right now to trust in Christ as your savior. Then, let's write in your Bible these words: 'Today, (date)_____, I confessed my sins to God and placed my faith in Christ to save me, signed _____.' That way you can always look back and know that today you did what the Bible says you need to do to have eternal life."

The idea is not original with me. This procedure is often called "driving a spiritual stake in the ground." But I believe this practice is also applicable to subject of forgiveness. Just as we need to be able to point to a time that we received God's forgiveness in our lives, we need to have a time fixed in our minds when we actually released another person from his offense against us. Whether or not you should verbalize your forgiveness to the offending party depends on the nature of the offense. But I believe we should always be able to point to a time when we have acknowledged to God (and ourselves) our forgiveness of the other person. Maybe you would want to write a formal release like this in your Bible or in your spiritual journal:

"In consideration of the forgiveness God has granted to

me, I forgive _____ of _____
       (person's name)                      (the offense)
on this date _____."

Whenever you are tempted to rehearse the pain of hurt you have experienced, you can always pull out your journal or open the flyleaf of your Bible and remember that you have formally released the other person from their debt.

## Trust in the Sovereignty of God

The only way to experience contentment with your life—your finances, your job, your family—is by believing in a sovereign God who has designed every detail of your life. We must believe that God's design and control of our lives extends to the hurts we experience. God can use our mistreatment by others for our ultimate good and for His eternal purpose. No one understood that truth better than the Old Testament character Joseph.

Joseph was one of the twelve sons of Jacob who was sold into slavery by his jealous brothers. Yet, through a series of miraculous circumstances, Joseph ascended to power in Egypt. He became Pharaoh's right-hand man. A great famine engulfed both Egypt and Canaan, where Joseph's family resided. Hearing that there was food in Egypt, Joseph's brothers traveled to Egypt to ask for food. Little did these men know that they would be making their appeal to the brother they had mistreated. How did Joseph respond to their request for food?

How would *you* respond if . . .

- your ex-wife, who had left you for someone else, asked you for money to repair her car she needed for her job?
- your coworker, who stabbed you in the back (and later lost his job), asked if he could use you for a reference on his résumé?
- your rebellious son, who said he hated you and never wanted to see you again, asked if he could live at home for a while until he could find another place to live?

When Joseph's brothers came to him begging for food, he had an opportunity for the kind of sweet revenge most of us could only dream about.

"Food? Funny you should mention that. Just yesterday I was thinking how much I had wanted food during those days I spent in that stinking pit you threw me into."

"But Brother Joseph, you don't understand, we are starving to death."

"Here is a quarter, guys. Go call someone who cares!"

But Joseph didn't respond that way. In fact, his attitude toward his brothers was nothing short of phenomenal. "Do not be afraid, for am I in God's place? And as for you, you meant evil against me, but God meant it for good in order to bring about this present result, to preserve many people alive" (Gen. 50:19–20). Joseph did not deny that his brothers had hurt him. He was quite honest in assessing their actions: "You meant it for evil." But Joseph did not focus on his brothers' actions or their motivations. Instead, he was able to see the hand of a sovereign God working through his brothers' evil actions: "But God meant it for good in order to bring about this present result, to preserve many people alive."

Think for a moment about how God used Joseph's brothers' treachery for a greater purpose. Because of what they did to Joseph, he ended up in Egypt where he became second in command to Pharaoh. And in that position, he was able to provide food for his family during the famine.

But the good did not stop there. Beyond Joseph's immediate family were in-laws and children who were saved as well. These seventy people formed the nucleus of the entire nation of Israel. From that nation, the Savior of the world was born—and you and I were delivered from the consequences of our sin. All of that because of an offense toward one man.

Think what would have happened if Joseph had reacted differently. Had Joseph become bitter against his brothers, failing to see the providence of God in the situation, he could have refused his brothers' request and allowed them to starve to death. The nation of Israel never would have been formed, the promise of a Savior would have been unfulfilled, and you and I would have been left to suffer the consequences of our sin.

Where did Joseph learn to forgive others and trust in God's sovereign purpose? I think he learned it from his father Jacob. Remember how Jacob refused to become bitter toward his uncle Laban and instead focused on what God was trying to accomplish in his own life? Jacob modeled that attitude of forgiveness for his sons.

As your sons and daughters watch you endure the mistreatment of others, what are they learning from you? "Don't get mad, get even," or "Father forgive them, for they know not what they do?" One of the best gifts you can leave your children is the ability to resist the trap of bitterness and to see God's hand working even through the hurts of others.

## FOR FURTHER REFLECTION

1. As you have thought about some of the hurts you have experienced from others, which one is most difficult for you to handle? Why?

2. Identify someone you know who has experienced a similar hurt. How could you use your experience to be an encouragement to that person?

3. How does recognizing your need for God's forgiveness motivate you to forgive others?

4. Which of the benefits of forgiveness is most appealing to you? Why?

5. Can you relate an example of how God has used the offense of another person for your good and for His purpose?

# CHAPTER NINE

## Seeing God's Hand in Your Mistakes

**M**istakes. We all make them. They are a part of "the road most traveled." Sometimes our mistakes can actually be stepping-stones to greater success. How many times have we heard a motivational speaker remind us that . . .

- Babe Ruth struck out 1,330 times and yet was considered one of the greatest baseball players of all time.
- George Bernard Shaw had his first five novels rejected.
- Thomas Edison discovered at least 1,800 ways not to build a lightbulb.
- Columbus thought he was discovering a shortcut to India when he discovered America.

Here is another illustration from our nation's history (source unknown):

At age 9, his mother died.

At 22, he lost his job as a store clerk. He wanted to go to law school, but lacked the education.

At 23, he went into debt to become a partner in a small store.

At 26, his business partner died, leaving him a huge debt that took years to repay.

At 28, after courting a girl for four years, he asked her to marry him. She said, "No."

At 37, on his third try, he was elected to Congress, but two years later, he failed to be reelected.

At 41, his four-year-old son died.

At 45, he ran for the Senate and lost.

At 47, he failed as the vice presidential candidate.

At 49, he ran for the Senate again, and lost.

At 51, he was elected President of the United States.

His name was Abraham Lincoln.

We are inspired by these stories because they remind us that our failures are not necessarily final. Mistakes can ultimately result in a happy ending. That's the American way.

But what happens when we see no positive results from our mistakes? How do we handle failures we seemingly will carry for the rest of our lives? I think about a close friend of mine who is certain that he will never be able to escape the consequences of his moral failure many years ago.

Tom and Becky married as soon as they graduated from college. The first few years of their marriage were filled with the typical problems of newlyweds—financial struggles, sexual adjustments, learning to give each other enough emotional space—but nothing too serious. However, during this period of time Tom was assigned to work on a project with three other people in his office. One of his coworkers was a woman with whom Tom developed instant rapport. Although she was not drop-dead gorgeous, Tom found Sara attractive. Initially there was no sexual chemistry between them. They shared a platonic friendship that included lunches together and sharing inside jokes with one another. Within a few months, Sara began to open up and confide in Tom about the marital difficulties she and her husband were experiencing. Tom assumed the role of "counselor" in the relationship and shared with Sara some of the lessons he had learned through his relationship with Becky.

One week Tom's boss dispatched the four-person task force to Chicago to observe a plant similar to their own. The second night of the trip, Tom heard a knock at his door. Sara was crying uncontrollably. He invited her in. She and her husband had exchanged some sharp words over the telephone.

You can guess the rest. An honest attempt at comforting Sara quickly degenerated into sex. Although both Tom and Sara were Christians, they were shocked by how little guilt they felt the next morning. Instead, they were exhilarated by the experience and made plans to repeat it the next night.

Tom and Sara spent the next four years of their lives lying to their respective spouses about sudden out-of-town business trips, mysterious credit card expenditures, frequent hang-up calls, and all the other evidences of a long-term affair.

Sara finally delivered her ultimatum to Tom: Leave Becky and marry her, or the affair was over. As cold as their marriage had grown, Tom still could not picture himself leaving Becky. Sara ended the relationship and went back to her husband.

Tom spent the next year in deep depression. The four-year affair had produced all kinds of memories that were hard to erase. The excitement of sneaking into an out-of-town hotel on a Friday night with Sara was replaced with sitting in silence with Becky at the local Mexican restaurant with so little to say. Tom had never felt more alone. In the first six years of married life he had managed to lose the love of not one, but two women who had meant everything to him.

Eventually, Tom confessed his moral failure to God. However, he felt his repentance was somewhat hypocritical since both he and God knew that had Sara not broken off the relationship, no repentance would had been forthcoming. Nevertheless, Tom's confession, coupled with the passing of time and the arrival of three children, has deadened the pain of his long-term affair with Sara.

Today, Tom and Becky, along with their three children, give the appearance of being a happy family. Tom is enjoying tremendous success in his business. He and Becky have a good—but not great—marriage. They are active in their local church. Yet, as Tom approaches his forty-fourth birthday, he finds himself asking the "what if" question more frequently about Sara. Not "what if I had left Becky for Sara"—he now realizes that would have been a catastrophic mistake, and he is grateful God spared him from making such a error. Instead, he is asking, "What if I had never invited Sara into my hotel room that night? What if I had invested those years improving my marriage with Becky? Would I . . .

- enjoy a better sex life with Becky than I do now?
- experience more of God's blessings in my life?
- be more successful in my career?
- have more friends than I do?"

As Tom enters his period of mid-life evaluation, he is beginning to feel that his affair with Sara was the major mistake that has tainted every other aspect of his life. Every time something bad happens to him—an investment turns sour, he and Becky have a violent argument, he loses out on a promotion—he secretly wonders if he is not being punished for his mistake. Tom has become a victim of regret.

## EVERYBODY MAKES MISTAKES

If we are going to experience contentment in our lives, we must make peace with every aspect of our life, including our own mistakes. We must believe that God can even use our wrong choices or moral failures for our ultimate good and for His eternal glory. In the last chapter, I asked you to picture someone who had hurt you deeply and to relive the pain of that offense so that you could apply the principles of forgiveness to a specific situation. Now, before we go any further, I would like you to recall a mistake you have made in your past. Your mistake might be:

- a bad investment that cost you a large portion of your retirement savings.
- a career change that did not work out like you thought it would.
- a painful divorce.
- a neglect of your children while they were young that has caused them to resent you in their teenage years.

As you recall the specific mistake that may have haunted you for some years, I imagine that it is a mistake that falls under one of these headings:

## Mistakes of Judgment

Every day we are bombarded with situations that require us to make a decision. You have a vacancy in your department at work and you have two equally qualified applicants for that position. You honestly can see little difference in the two. You wish you could wait to see if another candidate surfaces, but the vacancy is diminishing the productivity of your department. You make an arbitrary choice, and six months later you are sure you hired the wrong person.

Or, you and your family move to a new city and must find a house to purchase. Your real estate agent shows you thirty homes but only two appeal to you. House "A" is smaller, but fits more in your budget. House "B" is larger than you thought you could afford, but your agent reminds you that the continued appreciation of your home would make your purchase a wise decision. So you take the plunge. Two years later a major chemical manufacturer announces the construction of a new plant one mile from your home. You do not want to put your family's health at risk, so you decide to sell. However, the value of your property has plummeted and you are forced to take a financial bath.

Sometimes just the fear of making a wrong decision becomes a self-fulfilling prophecy. Dr. Roch Parayre, a teacher of business strategy at Southern Methodist University, asks his students if they would rather take a guaranteed $500,000 or a 95 percent chance for $10 million? Do you want to guess what choice most people make? Surprisingly, most choose the $500,000, even though the strong odds would make the $10 million the better choice. Why? "Because we will forgo a significant amount of money to avoid a little regret," Dr. Parayre observes.[1]

## Mistakes of Morality

In some ways, mistakes of judgment are easier to deal with than mistakes involving moral choices. "I carefully checked the references of candidate "A" and asked him every question under the sun. How could I have known he would turn out to be a loser?" Or, "How could I have known that chemical plant would move in down the street from me?" However, the knowledge that my mistake, and the resulting consequences, are purely the result of premeditated sin becomes a difficult emotional load to carry. As much as he tried to rationalize his affair with Sara, Tom knew that ultimately it was *his* choice. Tom now feels doomed to a mediocre marriage and tepid spiritual life because of his mistake.

Tom can probably identify with Moses. In an instant Moses allowed his temper to get the best of him, and he found himself on the backside of the desert, running for his life. He could blame no one for his failure but himself. F. B. Meyer wrote these words about Moses and his self-inflicted wound: "This is the bitterest of all—to know that suffering need not have been. It has resulted from inconsistency and indiscretion. That it is the result of one's own reaping and sowing. That the vulture that feeds on the vitals is the nestling of one's own rearing. Ah, me, this is pain."[2]

## Mistakes of "Asset Allocation"

The new catchphrase in money management today is "asset allocation." The idea is this: The maximization of your investments is more dependent on the proper mix of your investments rather than on the particular stock or bond you choose. It is more important that your investments are properly allocated between growth stocks, international equities, bonds, and precious metals, than that you chose the right stock or the right bond. You must allocate your resources properly.

Investment experts also tell us that we can only accurately judge our portfolio's performance over the long haul. Although your investment mix may produce a loss this year, it may more than make up for that loss in the next five years. Conversely, one winning year is no guarantee that your investments will produce positive results for the long-term.

The idea of asset allocation is a good metaphor for life itself. We must constantly choose how we are going to allocate our time, our energy, and our financial resources. What percent of our resources should we invest in our career, family, civic responsibilities, spiritual life, friendships, or our own health? These choices are critical and can have long-term implications. Unfortunately, like our financial portfolio, we can make the wrong "asset allocations" in our life and not realize it until it is too late. What makes these mistakes particularly painful is that they seem irreversible. Consider the person who . . .

- forfeits a college education to begin a business that ultimately fails.
- never exercises and at age fifty-five is diagnosed with heart disease.
- mortgages his family for his career only to be forced into early retirement.

Whenever I think about asset allocation, I am reminded of Lee Atwater, the take-no-prisoners political strategist responsible for George Bush's victory over Michael Dukakis in 1988. At the height of his career, Atwater was diagnosed with an inoperable brain tumor. As he approached his death in 1991, he wrote these words in an essay published by *Time* magazine:

> The '80s were about acquiring—acquiring wealth, power, and prestige. But you can acquire all you want and still feel empty. What power wouldn't I trade for a little more time with my family? What price wouldn't I pay for an evening with friends?

It took a deadly illness to put me eye to eye with that truth, but it is a truth that the country, caught up in its ruthless ambitions and moral decay, can learn on my dime. I don't know who will lead us through the '90s, but they must be made to speak to this spiritual vacuum at the heart of American society, this tumor of the soul."[3]

Lee Atwater came to understand the importance of asset allocation—only after it was almost too late for any changes.

## THE ROAD TO PEACE

I don't know under which of these three categories best describes the mistake you have in mind. But I do know this: Unless you are on your deathbed about to draw your last breath, it is not too late to make some meaningful changes in your life. However, to instigate lasting change we must first acknowledge and then make peace with our own mistakes. How do we do that? I believe there are five nonnegotiable steps to seeing God's hand in our mistakes.

### Acknowledge Your Mistake

Mistakes are like the hurts we discussed in the last chapter. Unless we first acknowledge their existence, we can never begin the road to emotional healing (remember the rattles in the car?) The Russian novelist Dostoyevsky described the inner turmoil of a murderer named Ilyon Raskolnikov in his masterpiece *Crime and Punishment.* Raskolnikov had brutally murdered a helpless old woman. Unable to bear the secret of his deed alone, he confessed his actions to a young girl named Sonia. She persuaded him to confess to the police, and he finally relented. He was sentenced to imprisonment in Siberia. Sonia followed him there, hoping that he would be able to forgive himself so that he could receive her love. But Raskolnikov could not forgive himself. Instead, he did what so many of us do—he tried to excuse himself. "Did not Napoleon do the same sort of thing, and do they not build him monuments?" he rationalized. Dostoyevsky wrote, "Oh, how happy he would have been if he could have blamed himself! He could have borne anything then, even shame and disgrace."[4]

There is a fine, but important, line between regret and repentance. It is possible, like Raskolnikov, to be extremely sorry for the consequences of our mistakes without ever admitting our error. Think about the story of King David in the Old Testament. David was a man whose mistake fell under the heading of "moral failure." Like Tom, he made the mistake of opening the door to immorality. His sin with Bathsheba went undiscovered for at least six months. During that time, David never could bring himself to acknowledge his sin to God or to man.

But denial could not erase the pain he felt. "When I kept silent about my sin, my body wasted away through my groaning all day long. For day and night Thy hand was heavy upon me; my vitality was drained away as with the fever heat of summer" (Ps. 32:3–4).

Whether your mistake was a bad decision, a poor choice, or an actual sin against God and/or others, it is important that you quit the blame game and acknowledge that you are the one who blew it.

### Accept Your Humanity

In my book *Guilt-Free Living* I describe "Big-Bird Theology." If you have a preschooler at home, you know what I am talking about. Whenever Big Bird, that giant yellow bird on "Sesame Street," makes a mistake, he has a standard reply: "Everybody makes mistakes." When my oldest daughter was three, she began to adopt that philosophy as a convenient rationalization for her disobedience. Whenever I confronted her about her misconduct, she would reply, "Well, Dad, *everybody* makes mistakes."

Accepting your humanity is not the same as the "Big Bird" approach to dealing with mistakes and outright sin. But there is something healthy—and biblical—about understanding our limitations. God does. The psalmist wrote, "So the LORD has compassion on those who fear Him. For He Himself knows our frame; He is mindful that we are but dust" (Ps. 103:13–14).

God created Adam and Eve as sinless individuals, but He was there in the garden when they chose to rebel. He understands how that propensity toward sin has been passed down from generation to generation. He realizes that sin is a part of every fiber of our being. That means we will never be perfect—not in this life, anyway. We are going to make mistakes—even bad mistakes. God understands that truth, but do *you?*

### Experience God's Forgiveness

Admitting and accepting our mistakes are important, but they are not enough. The most important step toward making peace with our past mistakes is to have the same attitude that God does about them. When we think of the word *sin,* we think of one of the "top ten" like murder, adultery, or theft. Yet the word *sin* actually means "to miss the mark." In its broadest sense, sin refers to our inability to experience perfection in each and every area of life. Thus, I believe we can expand the concept of sin to include our bad decisions and poor choices, along with our moral failures.

How does God view our mistakes? Let's allow God's Word to answer that question:

> As far as the east is from the west, so far has He removed our transgressions from us. (Ps. 103:12)
> He will again have compassion on us; He will tread our iniquities under foot. Yes, Thou wilt cast all their sins into the depths of the sea. (Mic. 7:19)
> "Blessed is the man whose sin the LORD will not take into account." (Rom. 4:8; cf. Ps. 32:2)

Each of those passages tells us that when we acknowledge our mistakes to God, He not only forgives us, but He forgets! One time I was counseling with a couple whose marriage had almost dissolved over the husband's unfaithfulness. Yet he was genuinely repentant and asked his wife's forgiveness. Her reply? "I may forgive you, but I will *never* forget." Translation: "You are going to be my slave for the rest of your life. If you don't fulfill my every desire, I am going to open my mental file, pull out your mistake, and remind you of what a louse you are."

But God does not store our offenses for future use. He does not "take into account" our sin. That phrase refers to an entry into an accountant's ledger. When you make a deposit at the bank, the teller (or now the automatic teller) records your deposit as a credit. When you withdraw money, your account is debited for the corresponding sum. However, once we have experienced God's forgiveness, our "debits" are erased. There is no longer a record of our mistakes. What a great truth!

Can you imagine going to your local ATM machine to get a balance on your checking account, only to discover your account has thousands of dollars more than you thought. When you inquire about it, the teller informs you that the bank accidentally erased all records of your expenditures for the last year. All they have a record of is your deposits!

That is what the Bible says about your mistakes. Once you have been forgiven, God no longer has a record of your sins. Why? Is God a sloppy bookkeeper? No, He is a perfect accountant. And every accountant knows that if the books are to balance, debits must be offset by credits.

God has offset the debits of our sins by the perfect righteousness of Jesus Christ. When you trust in Jesus Christ to be your savior, God takes the perfection of His Son and adds it to your account. Your sins have been offset by the righteousness of Christ. That is the spiritual transaction Paul has in mind when he writes, "But to the one who does not work, but believes in Him who justifies the ungodly, his faith is reckoned as righteousness" (Rom. 4:5).

Richard Hoefler tells a memorable story about a little boy who was given a slingshot while visiting his grandmother. One day he decided to engage in some target practice in the woods. Finding it difficult to hit the bull's-eye, he decided he needed a bigger target.

As he returned to the backyard, Grandma's pet duck waddled by. The boy took careful aim at the duck, released the sling shot and . . . *pow!* Direct hit. The duck fell dead, and the boy panicked. He quickly hid the dead duck in the woodpile, only to look up and see his older sister watching the entire escapade. Sally kept her mouth shut—at first. But after dinner that night, Grandma said to Sally, "Let's wash the dishes." Sally replied, "But Johnny said *he* wanted to wash the dishes, didn't you, Johnny?" Then she whispered to him, "Remember the duck!" So he did the dishes.

The next day Granddad invited the kids to go fishing. But Grandma said, "Sally and I need to stay home and help fix supper." Sally smiled and said, "That's taken care of. Johnny wants to stay home and help." Again Sally whispered to her brother, "Remember the duck." So Johnny stayed home.

This went on for several days until Johnny could not stand it any longer. With many tears, he confessed to his grandmother what had happened. "I know all about it, Johnny" she said giving him a hug. "I was standing at the kitchen window and saw the whole thing. Because I love you so much, I instantly forgave you. But I wondered how long you would let your sister make a slave of you."

Refuse to allow your mistakes to enslave you any longer. Instead, confess your mistakes to God and believe that through the perfect life and the sacrificial death of Jesus Christ, your mistakes have been forgiven and forgotten.

### View Your Mistakes as Learning Opportunities

I love the story I heard Ted Engstrom tell one time about a young executive who was about to become the president of a bank. He went to his predecessor who had led the bank for the past thirty years to see if he could glean any wisdom from him.

"Sir, will you tell me the key to success in the banking industry?"

"Son, I can answer that in two words: good decisions."

"That's great, Sir, but how do you make good decisions."

"I can answer that in one word: experience."

"But, sir, I'm just starting out. How can I gain the experience to make good decisions."

"Two words: *bad* decisions!"

The wisest man who ever lived offered this insight about the value of mistakes: "He whose ear listens to the life-giving reproof will dwell among the wise. He who neglects discipline despises himself, but he who listens to reproof acquires understanding" (Prov. 15:31–32).

Mistakes are inevitable. At some point you are going to hire the wrong person, invest in a losing stock, forfeit a great opportunity, or rebel against God's laws. And you will suffer some consequences for your actions. But instead of wallowing in self-pity over your mistake—or worse, instead of repeating it—learn from your mistake.

A manager at IBM once made a mistake that cost the company ten million dollars. The manager went to the president's office and offered his resignation. To his surprise, the president refused to accept the resignation. "I've just invested ten million dollars in your education. I'm not about to let you go now. Get back to work!" One important step in seeing God's hand in your mistakes is to view those mistakes as learning opportunities that may prevent bigger errors in the future.

### Trust in the Sovereignty of God

As we saw in the life of Joseph, God can use the wrong actions and motivations of others for our good and for His eternal purpose. If that is true, why should we be surprised that God can also use *our* wrong actions and motivations for our good and for His purpose.

Let's return to Moses for a moment. Remember how he killed that Egyptian in cold blood? Did God cause Moses to murder the soldier? Of course not. Moses sinned against God and he spent the next forty years in the desert paying for his mistake. Yet, in some inexplicable way, God used Moses' mistake to achieve His ultimate purpose. In the desert Moses learned valuable lessons about trusting in God that would prepare him for his future assignment. Meanwhile, back in Egypt, God was preparing both the Egyptians and the Israelites for the exodus. And at just the right time, God sent Moses back to Egypt to be the leader of God's people.

I don't begin to understand how God can use our wrong actions to achieve His purpose, but I know that He does.

One of my closest friends was once accused by his supervisor of organizing a one-day strike to protest the company's unfair dismissal of a fellow employee. One Tuesday evening, employee after employee called in sick with amazingly similar symptoms. The executives of the company were certain that Dan was the culprit behind the scheme. They threatened to fire him, which would have negatively impacted his career forever.

Fortunately, Dan was able to prove that he had been out-of-town that Tuesday evening. His job was salvaged. But where had he been? "Let's just say, it was somewhere a Christian had no place being," he confessed to me. Although the incident occurred many years ago, Dan still wonders how God orchestrated the events of that particular day. Dan made a mistake—he sinned—yet God used that mistake for his protection.

The most important key to making peace with our past mistakes is to trust in a God who is powerful enough to use our wrong decisions, poor choices, and even our outright rebellion for His purpose. I can't understand how a holy God can work through my mistakes, but I am grateful that He does. Aren't you?

## FOR FURTHER REFLECTION

1. What kind of mistake do you seem most prone to make: mistakes of judgment, morality, or "asset allocation"? Why?

2. If there is one mistake in your life you would erase, what would it be?

3. Using some of the Scripture passages cited in this chapter, describe how God views that mistake.

4. Relate three important lessons you have learned from your mistakes.

5. Can you recount an experience where God used one of your mistakes for good?

# CHAPTER TEN

## Seeing God's Hand in Your Death

A ccording to an old legend, one day a merchant in Baghdad sent his servant to the market. Soon the servant returned, white as a sheet and trembling. "What is wrong?" the master inquired. "While in the crowded market I felt a woman tugging at me. When I turned around I saw that she was Death. She looked at me and made a threatening gesture. Master, I beg you, lend me your horse so that I may hasten away to avoid her. I shall ride to Samaria and hide. Surely, she will not find me there."

The merchant lent his servant the horse and off he rode in great haste. Later that day the merchant went down to the marketplace and saw Death standing in the crowd. He approached her and asked, "Why did you frighten my servant this morning? And why did you make a threatening gesture?" Death answered, "I did not mean it as a threatening gesture. It was only a gesture of surprise. I was astonished to see your servant in Baghdad, for I have an appointment with him tonight in Samaria."[1]

I thought of this story yesterday as I stood over the corpse of a close friend and coworker who had died suddenly of a massive heart attack. As I gazed into the still-opened eyes of the body lying in the Coronary Care Unit, a flood of "if only's" filled my mind:

- If only he had heeded the warning signs that telegraphed his heart attack a few days earlier.
- If only he had been taken to a hospital with a better cardiac unit.
- If only he had not undergone the trauma of a shoulder operation a few months earlier.
- If only he had lost those extra pounds.
- If only he had not been under such intense pressure at work.

As friends and family members gathered in the family waiting area, you could hear many of the same sentiments being voiced in hushed conversations. But there was another thought that was not being articulated but was equally evident from peoples' expressions and behavior: "This could have been *me.*"

I know that this is going to sound like a cynical observation, but twenty years of ministry have led me to conclude that much of the shock and anguish at funerals is not over the dearly departed but over the realization of one's own mortality. The death of a friend or family member is a fresh reminder of the uncertainty, brevity, and fragility of life—a reminder that no one welcomes.

Men in their mid-life years have a particularly difficult time accepting their own mortality. I have found it fascinating to observe the reaction of my closest colleagues (all in their early to mid-forties) to our friend's death. One man is making sure that his will is in order. Another slightly overweight coworker pushed away dessert at lunch today. And me? I exercised an extra ten minutes today to compensate for the dessert I *didn't* push away. But no one really wants to talk about our friend's death. It hits too close to home. Dr. Daniel Levinson explains why. "For many reasons, then, at age 40 a man knows more deeply than ever before that he is going to die. He feels it in his bones, in his dreams, in the marrow of his being. His death is not simply an abstract, hypothetical event. An unpredictable accident or illness could take his life tomorrow. Even another thirty years does not seem so long: more years now lie behind than ahead."[2]

Maybe you find yourself thinking more frequently about death than you used to. Possibly, like me, you have stood on the cemetery plot where you will one day be buried and contemplated how brief life really is. A close friend's heart attack, a car accident, or the loss of a parent may have made your inevitable death more than an "abstract hypothetical event."

The growing realization of your mortality is not morbid, but is beneficial if you are going to discover contentment, as well as make the necessary corrections in your mid-life reevaluation. To quote Dr. L. Nelson Bell, missionary and father-in-law of Billy Graham, "Only those who are prepared to die are really prepared to live."[3] In this chapter we are going to see how a man can make peace with, and actually benefit from, the certainty of his death.

## THE BIBLICAL VIEW OF DEATH

The inevitability of death is a theme that appears like a flashing beacon throughout the Bible. We could spend the entire chapter (or book) studying the biblical view of death. But let me summarize three key themes about death in the Bible:

### Death Is Certain . . . Accept It

Lifespans have increased dramatically over the last century. Better diets and more advanced medical technology are largely responsible for lengthening our years. But there is a downside to increased longevity. Medical advancements have given many people a false sense of immortality. We live as if we will never die. George Will, in his review of Sherwin Nuland's book *How We Die,* writes, "Progress . . . has whetted appetites for unlimited progress toward retarding senescence and preserving youthfulness. . . . Too bad. Medicine has a job to do, but nature does too, and will do it, medicine be damned. Nature's job is to send us packing so that subsequent generations can flourish. And medicine that does not respect limits set by nature can make death unnecessarily unpleasant, and can distort life too."[4]

Will asserts that society's inability to accept death is illustrated by the fact that 80 percent of Americans die in hospitals, "tangled in webs of wires and tubes in intensive care units which are 'the purest form of our society's denial of the naturalness, and even necessity of death.'" But long before Will or Nuland ever wrote a sentence, the wisest man who ever lived reminded us of the inevitability of death for all of us: "It is the same for all. There is one fate for the righteous and for the wicked; for the good, for the clean, and for the unclean; for the man who offers a sacrifice and for the one who does not sacrifice. . . . This is an evil in all that is done under the sun, that there is one fate for all men" (Eccl. 9:2–3).

One reason I enjoy the Book of Ecclesiastes is because of Solomon's stark honesty. He doesn't try to sugarcoat the truth. Like it or not, you are not going to get out of this world alive. It doesn't matter whether you are a Christian or an atheist, you are going to die. To press this truth home with people, I sometimes have my congregation repeat this phrase out loud and in unison. Why don't you try it?

> I am going to die.

Say it again.

> I . . . Am . . . Going . . . To . . . Die!

Now, once more, at the top of your lungs.

> I . . . AM . . . GOING . . . TO . . . DIE!

Now, wasn't that uplifting? Seriously, even though you may not find those words on a Hallmark card, there is something healthy about realizing that you will not live forever. And that leads to a second truth the Bible presents about death.

## Life Is Brief . . . Treasure It!

Imagine that at the beginning of every day, someone placed in your bank account $1,440. The only catch is that you have to spend that money today. Whatever is left over cannot be carried over to the next day. Furthermore, this benevolent benefactor might stop his daily deposits at any moment. How would you respond? You would certainly make sure that you spent all of your money each day. And you would probably buy the things you wanted most first, knowing that the flow of cash could stop at any moment.

You can see where I am going with this. At the beginning of every day God deposits 1,440 minutes into our account. All of us, rich or not so rich, famous or not, receive the same number of minutes. Furthermore, we cannot carry over any of those minutes to the next day. We can't say, "I don't think I'll use my time today, I would like to redeposit it for further use." There is no guarantee that those daily deposits will continue.

Rabbi Harold Kushner speaks of the "instant coffee theory of life." He says that when you open a new jar of coffee (and can anything beat the taste of that first cup from the new jar?), you tend to dole out generous portions, because you have a full jar. But about halfway down the jar, you tend to be a little more conservative. By the time you reach the bottom of the jar, you find yourself measuring very carefully, reaching into the corners of the jar for every last grain.

We tend to treat our time in the same way. When we are young, we are careless about how we spend our time. We have our entire lives in front of us. Somewhere in those mid-life years, however, we realize we are not going to live forever, and we begin to reevaluate our priorities. By the time we reach our sixties and seventies we wonder, "Where did all the time go?"

Maybe that was what Moses was asking when, as an old man, he penned Psalm 90. He wrote that our lives are like "grass which sprouts anew. In the morning it flourishes, and sprouts anew; toward evening it fades and withers away" (Ps. 90:5–6). In reality, grass does not grow and die in a single day. Yet Moses is saying that, compared to eternity, our lives begin and end in less than a day. Maybe that is what James had in mind when he wrote, "You are just a vapor [literally, "a mist"] that appears for a little while and then vanishes away" (James 4:14).

What is Moses' response to the brevity of life? Panic? Depression? A regimented diet and exercise program? I like the way the *Living Bible* translates his conclusion in Psalm 90:12: "Teach us to number our days and recognize how few they are; help us to spend them as we should." I doubt Moses was a caffeine addict, but he said we should measure out our time as carefully as we might apportion the final grains in a near-empty coffee jar.

### Judgment Is Coming . . . Prepare for It

Our time on earth is brief, no doubt about it. How quickly our children grow up and leave home. How suddenly illness or accidents strike and take a loved one from us. How soon we find that we are no longer ascending in our careers, but preparing for our retirement years. The fact that life is short leads to two seemingly contradictory conclusions in Scripture. Solomon says that the inevitability of death should lead us to "Go then, eat your bread in happiness, and drink your wine with a cheerful heart. . . . Enjoy life with the woman whom you love all the days of your fleeting life. . . . Whatever our hand finds to do, verily, do it with all your might" (Eccl. 9:7, 9–10). Translation: You only go around once in life, so you had better grab all the "gusto" you can get. (I scored a lot of points with the men in my congregation when I paraphrased Solomon's advice: "Go home and make love as often as you can with your wife, for there will be no sex in heaven!")

Some Christians try to dismiss Solomon's conclusions as the observations of a man out of fellowship with God. I disagree. The wisest man who ever lived correctly observed that regardless of what awaits us in eternity, we all only have one chance at life on this planet, so we had better maximize it.

Solomon balances this truth with another truth: God will one day judge every person. "Rejoice, young man, during your childhood, and let your heart be pleasant during the days of young manhood. And follow the impulses of your heart and the desires of your eyes. Yet know that God will bring you to judgment for all these things. For God will bring every act to judgment, everything which is hidden, whether it is good or evil" (Eccl. 11:9; 12:14). The brevity of life should motivate us to prepare for our judgment before God. For non-Christians, that means making sure they have trusted in Christ and had their names written in the Lamb's book of life. For Christians, preparing for judgment means making sure that we invest our lives in furthering God's kingdom so that when we stand before the judgment seat of Christ our works are not labeled as worthless (see 2 Cor. 5:10).

## LIVING IN THE PRESENT

Death is certain . . . life is brief . . . judgment is coming. These are all important truths to believe. But how do I apply these truths to my everyday life? Allow me to suggest four positive decisions that every man should make in light of his approaching death.

### Practice "No-Regret" Living

The summer before I went to college, I traveled to Los Angeles for a week-long conference. Since my father worked for an airline, I was able to travel inexpensively on an airline pass. When I arrived at DFW airport, I discovered that I would be traveling on a new jumbo jet called the 747. Being an aviation buff, I knew that the 747 had a special first-class section on the second level of the giant aircraft. I was anxious to sit in the first-class section, but my ticket was for coach. So I asked the ticket agent what it would cost to upgrade my ticket to first-class. "Twelve dollars," he answered. I mulled the decision over and concluded that was too much money just to sit in the front of the plane, so I went coach. Wise decision? Hardly.

For the last twenty years, every time I see by a 747 I say to myself "If only I had upgraded my ticket. I will probably never have an opportunity again to fly first-class in a 747 so cheaply." I doubt that when I am on my deathbed I will say, "I am *so* glad I didn't waste that twelve dollars when I was eighteen years old." But I will always regret passing up an opportunity to do something I have always wanted to do.

At first I was hesitant to use that example, because it seemed so . . . well . . . insignificant. But as I have shared that story with several men, they have all nodded and replied, "Let me tell you *my* great regret in life." Sometimes the regret involved a missed experience; other times it involved a relationship taken for granted. One parent sent this letter to a local newspaper after the death of a son:

> Today we buried our 20-year-old son. He was killed instantly in a motorcycle accident on Friday night. How I wish I had known when I talked to him last that it would be the last time. If I had only known I would have said, "Jim, I love you and I'm so very proud of you."
>
> I would have taken the time to count the many blessings he brought to the lives of the many who loved him. I would have taken time to appreciate his beautiful smile, the sound of his laughter, his genuine love of people.
>
> When you put all the good attributes on the scale and you try to balance all the irritating traits such as the radio which was always too loud, the haircut that wasn't to our liking, the dirty socks under the bed, etc. . . . the irritations don't amount to much.
>
> I won't get another chance to tell my son all I would have wanted him to hear, but other parents, you do have a chance. Tell your young people what you want them to hear if you knew it would be your last conversation. . . .
>
> If there is any purpose at all to Jim's death, maybe it is to make others appreciate more of life and to have people, especially families, take the time to let each other know just how much we care.
>
> You may never have another chance. Do it today![5]

Let me make two practical suggestions to help you apply this principle of "no-regret" living so that when you approach the final hour of your life, you will not have a long list of "if onlys" that flood your mind:

*Make a list of ten things you want to do before you die and regularly refer to your list.* Several months ago, management expert Bobb Biehl allowed me to look through the notebook he carries with him everywhere. This notebook is the most elaborate organizational system I have ever seen. In addition to a monthly calendar, he has all kinds of lists packed into that notebook—lists of his top ten clients, friends, and phone numbers by geographical areas that he can call whenever passing through a nearby airport, outlines for books he wants to write, accomplishments in his life that are milestones for him.

But the list that really caught my attention was of those things he wants to do before he dies. Some of the items in the list fall under the category of "spiritual." Others could be labeled as professional accomplishments. Some may even seem trivial—the style of clothes he would like to wear or trips he would like to take. But I believe that Bobb's list—and his resolve to act on it—ensures that he will have few regrets when he approaches life's final hour.

*Keep in close contact with the important people of your life.* I was eating lunch with a man the other day who reminded me of the importance of maintaining relationships. He said that he and his best friend in college were inseparable. After college, their individual careers led them to different cities, but they were diligent to keep up with one another. "Eight years ago, my friend moved to the city where I am living. Even though we live only five minutes away from one another, we haven't talked in three years. Our lives have just gone in different directions." I could tell by the tone of his voice that he regretted this dissolution of his friendship, but he is not really sure what he could have done differently.

It takes effort and sometimes money to keep relationships alive. (My long distance phone bill is so high that MCI sends me a personalized Christmas card every year.) But I believe the expenditure of energy and finances to preserve and enrich our relationships is an important step in "no-regret" living. Stephen Levine writes, "If you were going to die soon and had only one phone call you could make, who would you call and what would you say? And why are you waiting?"[6]

## Make the Necessary Preparations for Your Death

William S. Spears, chairman of Energy Education, Inc., has a saying: "Success without succession is failure." Instead of paralyzing us with fear, the certainty of our death should motivate us to make certain that our families will be adequately cared for when we do depart this planet. I have seen the following scenario played out more times than I care to remember. A man dies without ever discussing his financial affairs, the location of his will (assuming he even has one), his desires for his funeral, or any other vital information with his wife and/or children. The result is that the family wastes energy that should be directed toward grief and recovery worrying about issues that should have been settled long ago.

Your death is another stop along "the road most traveled." As Tony Campolo says, "One of these days you are going to die, they're going to drop you in a hole, throw dirt in your face, and go back to the church to eat potato salad." One powerful way to experience contentment with your mortality is to make certain that you have made the necessary preparations for your family. Consider the following article by Audrey Hindle:

### A Husband's Final Gift

It was the Monday morning after Easter, the first day of spring vacation. I had decided to sleep in. My husband Jim, came in at 5:30 to kiss me good-bye. He was off to the local college campus to run and work out, his usual routine three times a week from November to May. Jim, a CPA and Certified Financial Planner, had been with his firm 20 years and followed through on most things he put his mind to, including exercise. Tax-season hours are grueling; workouts helped relieve the stress.

Neither of us knew that this was the day Jim would put into practice a principle he had long advocated.

A few years ago Jim wrote an article . . . "Leaving Your House In Order" in which he described how a husband could organize a letter or notebook to leave for his wife and family in the event of his death. To support this idea he cited 1 Timothy 5:8, "If anyone does not provide for his relatives, and especially for his immediate family, he has denied the faith and worse than an unbeliever," and 2 Kings 20:1, "Put your house in order, because you are going to die."

Urging husbands to get their financial house in order, Jim described how to list assets and liabilities, including checking accounts, stocks, bonds, CDs, IRAs, pensions, real estate, life insurance policies, and annuities. The notebook, he said, should include obituary information and a list of advisors, such as the attorney, accountant, banker and stockbroker. Most of these are not addressed in a will. A wife will need these details to take over family operations while she is overcome with grief.

At 7:15 A.M. the phone rang. Ryan, our 16-year-old-son, and I both answered. The voice told us Jim had collapsed at the college track and been brought to the emergency room. Would I come?

. . . I slowly absorbed the fact my husband was dead. Everyone else started to cry; I was too numb. I thought about all I needed to do, people I had to contact. My mind played hopscotch, jumping from one thought to another. What would I do with memories from 21 years of marriage? I was a widow at 43!

But suddenly I felt incredible peace. Jim was with the Lord and with our son . . . who had died 2½ years earlier at age 17 after a long battle with leukemia.

On Easter evening, Jim had taken the black notebook downstairs to show his Crown Ministries study group. Jim had said, "If I should die tomorrow, this book would tell my wife what to do, when to do it, and who to contact." Less than 12 hours later, at the young age of 45, he was dead.

Eight days after Jim's death, with book in hand, I went to see our lawyer. After looking at the book, he shook his head and said, "This is incredible."

A wife needs to feel secure. Jim demonstrated love, godly character and integrity by leaving a part of himself in his book. I have never felt abandoned or insecure. My husband took good care of us in his life, and is still taking care of us in his death.[7]

## Make the Necessary Spiritual Preparations for Your Death

Many of my friends in their mid-life years find themselves waking up more frequently in the middle of the night. Sometimes it is concern about work or even anxieties about death that interrupt their slumber. One man said to me, "I have concluded that whenever I wake up in the middle of the night, God has something He wants to talk to me about, and I had better listen!"

Jesus once told a story about a man who suffered from insomnia. But instead of listening to the voice of God, this man used the night hours to turn over the endless possibilities about how he could stockpile his increasing wealth. However, there is one contingency he never planned for—his own death. "But God said to him, 'You fool! This very night your soul is required of you; and now who will own what you have prepared?' So is the man who lays up treasure for himself, and is not rich toward God" (Luke 12:20–21).

Having your financial house in order when you die is important, but the greatest tragedy of all is to die without having made the necessary spiritual preparations. In the hour of our inevitable death, the only issue that really matters is our relationship with God. Jesus said, "Nevertheless do not rejoice in this, that the spirits are subject to you, but rejoice that your names are recorded in heaven" (Luke 10:20). Make sure, Jesus advises, that your name is recorded in the book of life before it is too late. The word translated *recorded* referred to the listing of a person's name on a census that indicated his eligibility to vote.

The other day I went to cast my vote in a local election. I brought my seven-year-old daughter, Julia, with me to give her a lesson in civic responsibility. When I approached the registrar at the desk, she asked for my name to check it against her list of eligible voters. While she hunted for my name, others in line shook my hand and told me how much they enjoyed watching me on television. I was glad my daughter got to hear the compliments.

"Dr. Jeffress," the woman interrupted, "I'm sorry, but your name is not on the list."

"It must be," I protested, "my wife voted here earlier today."

"Oh, her name is right here on the list, but yours isn't. You must not have sent in your voter's registration card."

Then I remembered what had happened. In all the confusion over our move several years ago, I kept postponing registering to vote. I had every intention of taking care of the matter, but other more pressing responsibilities took precedence.

My not-so-long-ago admirers in line scowled at me. My daughter was embarrassed over all the fuss. Another woman behind the desk started laughing and saying in a voice that everyone could hear, "Wait until I tell my friends that the pastor of the First Baptist Church forgot to register to vote!"

My humiliation that day pales in comparison to the shock many people face on judgment day when they discover that their names are not recorded in the book of life. The fact that the names of our family members are listed will not make any difference. No amount of pleading or bargaining will change God's mind. The Bible states that "if anyone's name was not found written in the book of life, he was thrown into the lake of fire" (Rev. 20:15). The fact that we will one day face God in judgment should be a powerful motivation to make sure we have trusted in Jesus Christ as our savior.

### Decide to "Die Well"

The phrase "die well" may sound like an oxymoron, but it comes from John Wesley's observation that all of his followers "died well." What did he mean? Those who have learned to "die well" do not approach the hour of their death with sorrow and horror, but with the anticipation of the wonderful future that awaits them in heaven. In his classic work *The Christian's Defense Against the Fears of Death,* Charles Drelincourt, Minister of the Protestant Church of Paris from 1620–1699, listed twelve "Consolations" that can prepare believers to "die well":

1. God will not forsake us in our grievous agonies.
2. Look upon God as a merciful Father and trust upon His infinite goodness.
3. Meditate continually upon the death and sufferings of our Lord Jesus Christ and trust upon the merits of His Cross.
4. Meditate often upon the Lord Jesus Christ in His sepulcher.
5. Meditate upon the Resurrection of our Lord Jesus Christ.
6. Meditate upon the Ascension of Jesus Christ into heaven and His sitting at the right hand of God.
7. Meditate upon our strict and inseparable union with Jesus Christ by His Holy Spirit and the fruits of His blessed immortality.
8. Consider that death delivers us from all temporal evils that we daily suffer.
9. Death delivers us from sin, which we may see reigning in the world, and from the remains of our corruption.
10. Meditate upon the glory and happiness of our souls at their departure out of the body.
11. Meditate upon the resurrection of our bodies.
12. Meditate upon the destruction of death and the eternal and most blessed life, which we shall enjoy both in soul and body after our resurrection.[8]

Drelincourt was simply saying that one key to experiencing contentment with our mortality is to meditate on God's sovereign purpose in our death.

Why is it important to learn the art of "dying well"? The statistic we saw earlier prove that most of us will not die accidental or unexpected deaths; but instead, we will deteriorate over a period of time. That means that our friends and families will watch us endure the process of dying. In fact, the final and most lasting impression we will make on those closest to us is how we die.

At the top of the list of all the things for which I thank my parents is teaching me how to die well. Both of my parents died prematurely, within a few years of one another. Oddly, the situations were almost identical. Each went into the hospital for exploratory surgery. In both cases, the doctors came out to the family waiting area to announce that they had discovered a malignancy that had metastasized and spread throughout the body. Each parent was predicted to live four months. And in each case, the parent died almost to the day of the doctors' prediction.

I had the opportunity to spend significant amounts of time visiting with my parents in the final days of their lives. Their faith in Christ never wavered, and they used their approaching deaths as a positive witness for Christ. A few weeks before my father died, I took him to visit with his attorney. When the meeting ended, my dad stood, shook hands with the lawyer, and said, "Jack, this is the last time I will see you here on earth. But I will meet you at the Eastern Gate in heaven."

My mom also modeled for me how to die well. In the final weeks before her death, she wrote this letter to her children which I read at her funeral:

*To My Children:*

*I could not bear to leave you if I were not sure that this separation is only temporary and that we shall spend all of eternity together. I thank God that you received Christ as your personal Savior when you were children and that you share these strong convictions with me, not because we hope that they are true, but because we know Truth.*

*I do not want you to live your lives eclipsed by any myths about me. Whatever has made my life worthwhile or valuable to you or anyone else is a direct gift to you from Christ through me. . . .*

*My casket will be closed because no one is there. To be absent from the body is to be present with the Lord, and I am with Christ, which is far better. I hope that you are able to celebrate my release.*

*Now about our meeting place: at church, it was by Miss Bertha's picture; at Northpark, it was at Kip's; at the State Fair, it was by Big Tex. I'll meet you again on that great resurrection morning in the very presence of our Lord Jesus Christ, Whom having not seen we love—but we'll know Him by those nail prints in His hand. Bring with you all who will come.*

*Thank you for exceeding my fondest expectations and for being my very best and most understanding friends.*

*With an everlasting love,*
*Your mother*

Many of the lectures and much of the advice my parents gave me have long since been forgotten. But I will never forget the invaluable lessons I learned from my parents about dying well.

I close with this observation my mom made in the last month of her life. Because of her notoriety as an outstanding journalism teacher, my mother's illness and death received much attention in the Dallas media. In fact, the day of her funeral the *Dallas Morning News* wrote their lead editorial about the impact my mother had made on the city. A few weeks before she died, a television station did an in-depth interview with her about her approaching death and later broadcast it the night she died. "Mrs. Jeffress," the interviewer asked, "how do you deal with the fact that your case is terminal and that there is no chance of recovery?" My mother's reply was classic. "Matt, we are *all* terminal. The only difference is some of us realize it, and some of us don't."

I have got some good news and some bad news for you. The bad news is that your case *is* terminal. The good news is that you still have time to make some mid-course corrections that will prepare you for death and for eternity.

## FOR FURTHER REFLECTION

1. If you live to age seventy-five, how many years do you have left? What percentage of your life has already been spent?

2. List five things you would like to do before you die. Beside each item, list the greatest obstacle to achieving that goal.

3. What are some practical ways you can prepare your wife and children for your death?

4. Do you feel at ease with the prospect of facing the judgment of God when you die? Why, or why not? What changes would you like to make in your relationship with God?

5. What would you *like* to have written on your tombstone? What do you think your family and closest friends will remember most about you when you die?

# CHAPTER ELEVEN

## Seeing God's Hand in Your Life

I once heard a preacher explain how he organized his sermons: "First, I tells the people what I's gonna tell 'em; then I tells 'em; and then, I tells 'em what I already done told 'em." Pretty effective pedagogy, I would say.

In this wrap-up chapter, I would like to employ the above educational principle by reviewing what we have seen along "the road most traveled."

## THREE OBSERVATIONS ABOUT OUR LIVES

### Most of Us Are Destined to Live Ordinary Lives

One man in his mid-life years summarized his attitude about life this way: "You have to understand that my generation entered adulthood with the assumption that we would all have good jobs that paid more each year, career tracks that had no limits, marriages that would never grow dull or troublesome, and bodies that would never fail us. I'm forty-two now. I've got friends who've been laid off of work, friends whose marriages are just plain awful, and friends who are having ulcers and heart attacks. A lot of us just don't know how to face all of this. We're just downright depressed."[1]

At the risk of adding to the depression some of you may be feeling, let me summarize the kind of ordinary lives most of us will experience:

- Most of us will earn ordinary incomes and never feel like we have enough money.
- Most of us will labor at jobs we do not enjoy for longer than we had planned and that offer little chance of promotion.
- Most of us will marry ordinary wives who, with our assistance, will produce ordinary children.
- Most of us will be deeply wounded by a significant person in our lives.
- Most of us will make at least one tragic mistake that will forever alter the direction of our life.
- *All* of us will die.

You can probably understand why one publisher responded to the idea for this book by saying, "This sounds like the most depressing book ever written. Why would any man want to read that they have been condemned to an ordinary life?" But just look at the men around you—you know what I have just written *is* the truth. But it is only *part* of the truth.

### God's Sovereignty Makes Our Ordinary Life Extraordinary

The only way to experience contentment with our "ordinary" lives is to trust in God's sovereign design for every aspect of our existence.

Once a month our church hosts a Power Lunch for 500–600 businessmen and businesswomen in our community. Recently, one of my associates spoke on a most unusual subject: "Everything I Know about Life I Learned from Cartoons." As he reviewed some of the classic Warner Brothers cartoons, he made the following observations about life:

*"If the bald-headed guy with the shotgun keeps showing up, wise up."* Bugs Bunny was a quick study. He learned that whenever Elmer Fudd showed up, he had better scram. Unfortunately, some people never learn from their mistakes. They are like the fool described in Proverbs 27:22: "Though you grind a fool in a mortar, grinding him like grain with a pestle, you will not remove his folly from him" (NIV).

*"Everyone has their share of thuffering thuccotash."* Like poor old Sylvester the Cat, we all have our share of problems. The good guy doesn't always win. But according to James 1:2–3, suffering is a part of God's plan for our spiritual maturity: "Consider it all joy, my brethren, when you encounter various trials, knowing that the testing of your faith produces endurance."

*"No matter how many times you fail, get blown up, fall off a cliff, or get an anvil dropped on you, don't give up."* Wyle E. Coyote may have never caught the Roadrunner, but you must admire his persistence (but why did he keep ordering all of that substandard junk from Acme?).

*"Whoever is drawing the picture has total control."* Perhaps the most valuable truth my associate learned from his cartoon viewing came from that renowned theologian Daffy Duck. Maybe you remember the cartoon in which the animated Daffy has an argument with his real-life animator about the direction of the story. The exchange gets pretty heated until the artist simply erases Daffy from the picture. End of argument. Daffy learned the hard way that the artist *always* has total control.

Many thousands of years ago there lived a man who had a similar argument with his Creator (fortunately, God doesn't always settle arguments with an eraser). He, like Daffy, did not like the way the storyline of his life was progressing. God's plan for Job included the loss of his assets, his children, and finally his health. Job's initial response to his situation was nothing short of remarkable: "Naked I came from my mother's womb, and naked I shall return there. The LORD gave and the LORD has taken away. Blessed be the name of the LORD" (Job 1:21).

However, when catastrophe strikes, our initial reaction does not always reveal our long-term response. Many times people confuse shock with spirituality. I imagine some of Job's friends initially commented, "Oh, isn't Job amazing? You would think that after losing his children, he would be angry at God. His faith is so strong." But the more Job contemplated his loss, the more he began to question God. Most people like to focus on Job's faith described in chapters 1–2; but few people want to consider his crisis of faith expressed in chapter 3:

> "Why is light given to him who suffers, and life to the bitter of soul;
> Who long for death, but there is none, and dig for it more than for hidden treasures. . . .
> For my groaning comes at the sight of my food, and my cries pour out like water.
> For what I fear comes upon me, and what I dread befalls me.
> I am not at ease, nor am I quiet, and I am not at rest, but turmoil comes." (Job 3:20–21, 24–26)

Job had serious questions he wanted answered. Yet, for the longest period of time, God was silent. When God finally chose to respond to Job's question, He refused to answer the "whys" of Job's suffering. Instead, God reminded Job of His sovereign control over the universe:

> "Who is this that darkens counsel by words without knowledge? Now gird up your loins like a man, and I will ask you, and you instruct Me!

"Where were you when I laid the foundation of the earth? Tell Me, if you have understanding, who set its measurements, since you know? . . .

"Have you ever in your life commanded the morning, and caused the dawn to know its place; that it might take hold of the ends of the earth, and the wicked be shaken out of it? . . .

"Is it by your understanding that the hawk soars, stretching his wings toward the south? . . .

"Will the faultfinder contend with the Almighty? Let him who reproves God answer it." (Job 38:2–5, 12–13; 39:26; 40:12)

For four chapters, God lectured Job on His power and wisdom. And yet, in His extended monologue, God never once answers the question "Why?" Frederick Buechner summarizes God's speech to Job this way: "God doesn't explain. He explodes. He asks Job who he thinks he is anyway. He says that to try to explain the kind of things Job wants explained would be like trying to explain Einstein to a little-neck clam. . . . God doesn't reveal his grand design. He reveals himself."[3] God's answer to Job's serious questions can be summarized in two words: "Trust me."

For the longest time, I avoided preaching on Job because I didn't like the ending of the story. The finale of Job's ordeal is so seemingly corny that it would make a Disney executive blush. After all of Job's suffering, God finally rewards Job with ten new children, and doubles his inventory of donkeys, sheep, and camels. Isn't life grand?

The conclusion of this story used to bother me because rarely does life turn out this way. I've seen too many people—good people—come to the end of their lives ill, penniless, and lonely to believe that Job's story is the norm for most believers. No wonder Job could express his confidence in God's plan, since that plan included great material reward: "I know that you can do anything and that no one can stop you. You ask who it is who has so foolishly denied your providence. It is I. I was talking about things I knew nothing about and did not understand, things far too wonderful for me" (Job 42:2–3, TLB).

Then someone pointed out to me a simple fact I had over-looked: Job voiced his trust in God's plan *before* God rewarded him. In the midst of tremendous material and emotional loss, Job still believed God was in control. Job had no way of knowing how his life would turn out—but regardless of his circumstances, Job trusted in God's sovereign plan for his life.

Job's words remind me of a more contemporary example of unconditional faith in God's plan. In the final years of his life, William Booth, founder of the Salvation Army, became desperately ill. His son Bramwell was given the assignment of telling his father that he would soon lose his eyesight. "You mean that I will be blind? I shall never see your face again?" "No, probably not in this world," his son answered. Booth's biographer continues, "During the next few moments the veteran's hand crept along the counter-pane to take hold of his son's, and holding it he said very calmly, 'God must know best!' And after another pause, 'Bramwell, I have done what I could for God and for the people with my eyes. Now I shall do what I can for God and for the people without my eyes.'"[3]

Whether God's plan for your life includes blindness, poverty, loneliness, or just plain "ordinary-ness," you will only find con-tentment with that plan when you understand and accept God's sovereignty over every aspect of your life.

In his novel *The Eighth Day,* Thornton Wilder weaves a story about a man whose life is destroyed by bad luck and hostility. Wilder refuses to offer the reader a happy ending to the story. Instead, he uses the image of a tapestry to explain his hero's life. If you view a tapestry from the right side, you will see an intricate piece of art consisting of threads of varying colors and lengths woven together to form a beautiful picture. But if you turn the tapestry over, you see a jumble of threads of varying lengths. Some are knotted; others are cut; still others go off in various directions. Wilder says that God has a pattern into which all of our lives fit. Some lives must be twisted, knotted, or cut short, while others are of impressive length. Why? Not because one thread is more deserv-ing than the other, but simply because God's pattern requires it.[4]

Your job, wife, children, financial status, and even the length of your life are just a part of an even bigger picture God has created. Some of you might rebel against the idea of a sovereign God who treats us as a simple piece of thread to fit into His plan. But the Bible reminds us that the Lord is not only a sovereign God with an eternal purpose, but He is also a loving God. There is never a contradiction between God's sovereignty over our lives and His deep love for us. David understood how God's love perfectly interfaces with His sovereignty when he wrote, "The Lord will work out his plans for my life—for your lovingkindness, Lord, continues forever. Don't abandon me—for you made me. . . . How precious it is, Lord, to realize that you are thinking about me constantly! I can't even count how many times a day your thoughts turn towards me. And when I waken in the morning, you are still thinking of me!" (Ps. 138:8; 139:17–18, TLB).

The message of *The Road Most Traveled* is that while most of us are destined to live an ordinary life, every detail of our life is a part of God's sovereign plan—a plan designed for our good and for God's eternal purpose.

But there is one final truth that we need to understand about our "ordinary life". . .

### Something Better Awaits Us

Think for moment how we would feel if our marriages were perfect, if our jobs totally fulfilled us, if we had all the money we ever needed, and if we went through life without experiencing any hurts or making any mistakes. Why then would we ever want to leave this earth? Yet throughout the Bible God reminds us that our residence here is only temporary. Our citizenship is not on earth, but in heaven. One way God keeps us from getting too attached to this life is by allowing us to experience an ordinary life so that we might hunger for something better.

I urge you not to fall for "the grass is greener" myth—especially during the time of your mid-life evaluation. God has designed every aspect of your life for your good and for His eternal purpose. Too many men have shipwrecked their lives in their quest for something better.

Yet there *is* something better. Philip Yancey writes, "The Bible never belittles human disappointment, but it does add one key word: temporary. What we feel now, we will not always feel. Our disappointment is itself a sign, an aching, a hunger for something better. And faith is, in the end, a kind of homesickness—for a home we have never visited but have never once stopped longing for."[5]

The unhappiness, unrest, and unfulfilled dreams we all experience from time to time remind us that we are not home yet. There is one more stop to anticipate along "the road most traveled."

## FOR FURTHER REFLECTION

1. If you could register one complaint with God about your life, what would it be?


2. Does the knowledge of God's sovereignty in your life comfort you or threaten you? Why?


3. Do you believe there are limits to God's control over your life? Explain.


4. Can you recall two or three times in your life when you unmistakably saw God's sovereignty demonstrated in your life?


5. What are you looking forward to most about heaven? Why?

# NOTES

## Chapter One: The Road Most Traveled

1. Harold Kushner, *When All You've Ever Wanted Isn't Enough* (New York: Pocket Books, 1986), 146.

2. Adapted from "The Station and Other Gems of Joy" by Robert J. Hastings. Used by permission.

3. James Dobson, as quoted in *Living on the Ragged Edge* by Charles R. Swindoll (Waco, Tex.: Word Publishing, 1985), 19.

## Chapter Two: Mid-Life Mess-Up

1. Nancy Mayer, *The Male Mid-Life Crisis* (New York: Penguin Books USA Inc., 1978), 19.

2. Ibid., 34–35.

3. Ibid., 22.

4. Daniel J. Levinson, *The Seasons of a Man's Life* (New York: Ballantine Books, a division of Random House, Inc., 1978), 26.

5. Hugh Prather, *Notes to Myself* (New York: Bantam Books, a division of Bantam Doubleday Dell Publishing Group, Inc.), 34.

6. Mike Royko, column syndicated by Tribune Media Services and published in *The Orlando Sentinel,* August 2, 1994, A–11.

7. Mayer, *Crisis,* 421.

## Chapter Three: The Best Place to Be . . . Is Wherever You Are

1. Steve Farrar, *Point Man* (Portland, Ore.: Multnomah Books, 1990), 160–61.

2. Russ Crosson, *A Life Well Spent* (Nashville: Thomas Nelson Publishers, 1994), 32.

3. Ibid., 34.

4. Nancy Mayer, *The Male in Mid-Life Crisis* (New York: Penguin Books USA Inc., 1978), 169.

5. Charles R. Swindoll, *Laugh Again* (Dallas: Word Publishing, 1991), 57.

6. "Count Your Blessings," by Johnson Oatman Jr. in *The Baptist Hymnal* (Nashville: Convention Press, 1975), 231.

Chapter Four: Seeing God's Hand in Your Finances

1. As quoted in *Choose Your Attitudes, Change Your Life* by Robert Jeffress (Wheaton, Ill.: Victor Books, 1992), 90. Permission granted by Ann Landers and Creators Syndicate.

2. Some of the ideas in this section adapted from *Choose Your Attitudes, Change Your Life,* 88–90.

3. Richard J. Foster, *The Challenge of the Disciplined Life* (San Francisco: HarperSanFrancisco, a division of HarperCollins Publishers, 1985), 29.

4. *Newsweek,* January 30, 1995, 42.

5. As quoted in *The Life God Blesses* by Gordon MacDonald (Nashville: Thomas Nelson Publishers, 1994), 43.

6. Ibid., 20–21.

7. Adapted from *Master Your Money* by Ron Blue (Nashville: Thomas Nelson Publishers, 1986), 77.

8. Joe Dominquez and Vicki Robin, *Your Money or Your Life* (New York: Viking, a division of Penguin Books USA Inc., 1992), 171.

9. Foster, *Disciplined Life,* 43–44.

10. Ibid., 55.

Chapter Five: Seeing God's Hand in Your Work

1. Chuck Colson and Jack Eckerd, *Why America Doesn't Work* (Dallas: Word Publishing, 1991), xii.

2. Gordon MacDonald, *Living at High Noon* (Old Tappan, N. J.: Fleming H. Revell Company, 1985), 126–27.

3. Joel Gregory, *Too Great a Temptation* (Fort Worth: The Summit Group, 1994), 126.

4. Daniel Levinson as quoted in MacDonald, *Living,* 123–24.

5. George Barna, *If Things Are So Good, Why Do I Feel So Bad?* (Chicago: Moody Press, 1994), 21–22.

6. Jeffrey K. Salkin, *Being God's Partner* (Woodstock, Vt.: Jewish Lights Publishing, 1994), 17.

7. These two truths about work are adapted from *Your Work Matters to God* by Doug Sherman and William Hendricks (Colorado Springs: NavPress, 1987), 81–83, 88–90.

8. As quoted in *Everything You've Heard Is Wrong* by Tony Campolo (Dallas: Word Publishing, 1992), 130–31.

9. Bobb Biehl, *100 Profound Questions* (Lake Mary, Fla.: Masterplanning Group International, 1995), 8–9.

10. As quoted in *A Life Well Spent* by Russ Crosson (Nashville: Thomas Nelson Publishers, 1994), 102.

11. Hughes, *Disciplines,* 130.

12. As quoted in *A Life Well Spent,* 53.

13. *U. S. News and World Report,* March 13, 1995, 53.

14. Bob Buford, *Halftime* (Grand Rapids: Zondervan Publishing House, 1994), 83.

Chapter Six: Seeing God's Hand in Your Spouse

1. Jim Conway, *Men in Mid-Life Crisis* (Elgin, Ill.: David C. Cook Publishing Company, 1978), 212–13.

2. Steve Farrar, *Point Man* (Portland, Ore.: Multnomah Books, 1990), 82.

3. J. Allan Petersen, *The Myth of the Greener Grass* (Wheaton, Ill.: Tyndale House Publishers, Inc., 1983), 188–89.

4. Pat and Jill Williams, *Rekindled* (Old Tappan, N. J.: Fleming H. Revell Company, 1985), 132.

5. Ibid., 138.

6. Petersen, *Grass,* 179–80.


## Chapter Seven: Seeing God's Hand in Your Children

1. Gordon MacDonald, *Living at High Noon* (Old Tappan, N. J.: Fleming H. Revell Company, 1985), 187.

2. Paul Lewis, *The Five Key Habits of Smart Dads* (Grand Rapids: Zondervan Publishing House, 1994), 17.

3. Ibid., 16.

4. Dr. Ralph Minear and William Proctor, *Kids Who Have Too Much* (Nashville: Thomas Nelson Publishers, 1989), 129.

5. Ibid.

6. The ideas in this section are adapted from *Kids Who Have Too Much,* 126–30.

7. Ken Davis, *How to Live with Your Kids When You've Already Lost Your Mind* (Grand Rapids: Zondervan Publishing House, 1992), 176.

8. Tim Hansel, *What Kids Need Most in a Dad* (Old Tappan, N. J.: Fleming H. Revell Company, 1984), 165–66.

9. Charles R. Swindoll, *Growing Wise in Family Life* (Portland, Ore.: Multnomah Press, 1988), 100.

10. Steve Farrar, *Point Man* (Portland, Ore.: Multnomah Books, 1990), 196.

11. Bill Hybels, *Honest to God* (Grand Rapids: Zondervan Publishing House, 1990), 89.


## Chapter Eight: Seeing God's Hand in the Hurts of Others

1. Lewis B. Smedes, *Forgive and Forget* (San Francisco: Harper and Row Publishers, 1984), 139–40.

2. Ibid., 126–27.

3. Frank B. Minirth and Paul D. Meier, *Happiness Is a Choice* (Grand Rapids: Baker Book House, 1978), 113.

4. Charles Stanley, *Forgiveness* (Nashville: Thomas Nelson Publishers, 1987), 158.

5. *Parade,* April 23, 1995, 5.

### Chapter Nine: Seeing God's Hand in Your Mistakes

1. *The Dallas Morning News,* April 30, 1995.

2. Author's file. Source unknown.

3. *The Dallas Morning News,* April 30, 1995.

4. Lewis B. Smedes, *Forgive and Forget* (San Francisco: Harper and Row Publishers, 1984), 73–74.

### Chapter Ten: Seeing God's Hand in Your Death

1. Charles Stanley, *Eternal Security* (Nashville: Thomas Nelson Publishers, 1990), 112.

2. Daniel J. Levinson, *The Seasons of a Man's Life* (New York: Ballantine Books, a division of Random House Inc.), 205.

3. Billy Graham, *Facing Death* (Waco, Tex.: Word Books, 1987), inside cover.

4. George Will, *Newsweek,* March 7, 1994.

5. Jack Canfield and Mark Victor Hansen, *A Second Helping of Chicken Soup for the Soul* (Deerfield Beach, Fla.: Health Communications, Inc., 1995), 159–60.

6. Ibid., 159.

7. Audrey Hindle, "A Husband's Final Gift," *Contact Quarterly* 53, no. 3, 30. Reprinted from CONTACT Quarterly published by Christian Business Men's Committee of USA, P.O. Box 3308, Chattanooga, TN 37404.

8. Herbert Lockyer, *Last Words of Saints and Sinners* (Grand Rapids: Kregel Publications, 1969), 223.

### Chapter Eleven: Seeing God's Hand in Your Life

1. Gordon MacDonald, *The Life God Blesses* (Nashville: Thomas Nelson Publishers, 1994), 9.

2. Philip Yancey, *Disappointment with God* (Grand Rapids: Zondervan Publishing House, 1988), 190.

3. MacDonald, *Life,* 65–66.

4. Harold S. Kushner, *When Bad Things Happen to Good People* (New York: Avon Books, a division of The Hearst Corporation, 1981), 17–18.

5. Yancey, *Disappointment,* 245–46.